Growing in the Gospel

The Psalms Project Volume Four

Discovering the Spiritual World through the Psalms – Psalm 31-40

Michael Harvey Koplitz

All Scripture quotations, unless otherwise noted, are taken from the New American Standard Bible®, Copyright © 1960, 1962, 1963, 1968, 1971, 1972, 1973, 1975, 1977, 1995 by the Lockman Foundation. Used by permission (www.Lockman.org)

The NASB uses italic to indicate words that have been added for clarification. Citations are shown with large capital letters.

TABLE OF CONTENTS

Psalm 31 7

Psalm 32 19

Psalm 33 31

Psalm 34 47

Psalm 35 63

Psalm 36 79

Psalm 37 89

Psalm 38 107

Psalm 39 121

Psalm 40 133

Appendix 149

The goal of this project:

This research project will examine the 150 psalms for the spiritual awareness each Psalm offers. Each Psalm will be examined by its language and the commentary of the Sages. The spiritual awareness analysis will be done in alignment with Ari's definition of the Tree of life, the Book of Creation, and the Zohar. Each verse of the Psalm will be rewritten using the intent of the language and spiritual commentary to convey its spiritual lesson.

The main resources:

> The Zohar
>
> The Book of Creation
>
> Ari's writing on the Tree of Life and the Ten Sefirot
>
> The Theological Wordbook of the Old Testament
>
> Samson Hirsch's commentary on the Psalms
>
> Tehillim – Psalms – A new translation with a commentary anthologized from the Talmudic and rabbinic sources
>
> Accordance Bible Software

Psalm 31

New American Standard 1995	Hebrew

Psa. 31:0 For the choir director. A Psalm of David.
 	
Psa. 31:1   *a*In You, O LORD, I have taken refuge;
    Let me never *b*be ashamed;
    *c*In Your righteousness deliver me.
2   *a*Incline Your ear to me, rescue me quickly;
    Be to me a *b*rock of ¹strength,
    A stronghold to save me.
3   For You are my ¹rock and *a*my fortress;
    For *b*Your name's sake You will lead me and guide me.
4   You will *a*pull me out of the net which they have secretly laid for me,
    For You are my *b*strength.
5   *a*Into Your hand I commit my spirit;
    You have *b*ransomed me, O LORD, *c*God of ¹truth.
 	
Psa. 31:6   I hate those who *a*regard ¹vain idols,
    But I *b*trust in the LORD.
7   I will *a*rejoice and be glad in Your lovingkindness,
    Because You have *b*seen my affliction;
    You have known the troubles of my soul,
8   And You have not *a*given me over into the hand of the enemy;
	לְמְנַצֵּחַ מִזְמוֹר Psa. 31:1
	לְדָוִד ׃ ² בְּךָ יְהוָה חָסִיתִי אַל־
	אֵבוֹשָׁה לְעוֹלָם בְּצִדְקָתְךָ
	פַלְּטֵנִי ׃ ³ הַטֵּה אֵלַי ׀ אָזְנְךָ
	מְהֵרָה הַצִּילֵנִי הֱיֵה לִי ׀ לְצוּר־
	מָעוֹז לְבֵית מְצוּדוֹת
	לְהוֹשִׁיעֵנִי ׃ ⁴ כִּי־סַלְעִי
	וּמְצוּדָתִי אָתָּה וּלְמַעַן שִׁמְךָ
	תַּנְחֵנִי וּתְנַהֲלֵנִי ׃ ⁵ תּוֹצִיאֵנִי
	מֵרֶשֶׁת זוּ טָמְנוּ לִי כִּי־אַתָּה
	מָעוּזִּי ׃ ⁶ בְּיָדְךָ אַפְקִיד רוּחִי
	פָּדִיתָה אוֹתִי יְהוָה אֵל אֱמֶת ׃ ⁷
	שָׂנֵאתִי הַשֹּׁמְרִים הַבְלֵי־שָׁוְא
	וַאֲנִי אֶל־יְהוָה בָּטָחְתִּי ׃ ⁸
	אָגִילָה וְאֶשְׂמְחָה בְּחַסְדֶּךָ אֲשֶׁר
	רָאִיתָ אֶת־עָנְיִי יָדַעְתָּ בְּצָרוֹת
	נַפְשִׁי ׃ ⁹ וְלֹא הִסְגַּרְתַּנִי בְּיַד־
	אוֹיֵב הֶעֱמַדְתָּ בַמֶּרְחָב רַגְלָי ׃
	¹⁰ חָנֵּנִי יְהוָה כִּי צַר־לִי עָשְׁשָׁה
	בְכַעַס עֵינִי נַפְשִׁי וּבִטְנִי ׃ ¹¹ כִּי

You have set my feet in a large place.

Psa. 31:9   Be gracious to me, O LORD, for [a]I am in distress;

My [b]eye is wasted away from grief, [c]my soul and my body *also*.

10   For my life is spent with [a]sorrow
And my years with sighing;
My [b]strength has failed because of my iniquity,
And [c]my [1]body has wasted away.

11   Because of all my adversaries, I have become a [a]reproach,
Especially to my [b]neighbors,
And an object of dread to my acquaintances;
Those who see me in the street flee from me.

12   I am [a]forgotten as a dead man, out of mind;
I am like a broken vessel.

13   For I have heard the [1a]slander of many,
[b]Terror is on every side;
While they [c]took counsel together against me,
They [d]schemed to take away my life.

Psa. 31:14   But as for me, I trust in You, O LORD,
I say, "[a]You are my God."

15   My [a]times are in Your hand;
[b]Deliver me from the hand of my enemies and from those who persecute me.

16   Make Your [a]face to shine upon Your servant;
[b]Save me in Your lovingkindness.

כָּלוּ בְיָגוֹן חַיַּי וּשְׁנוֹתַי בַּאֲנָחָה
כָּשַׁל בַּעֲוֺנִי כֹחִי וַעֲצָמַי עָשֵׁשׁוּ׃
12 מִכָּל־צֹרְרַי הָיִיתִי חֶרְפָּה
וְלִשֲׁכֵנַי ׀ מְאֹד וּפַחַד לִמְיֻדָּעָי
13 רֹאַי בַּחוּץ נָדְדוּ מִמֶּנִּי׃
נִשְׁכַּחְתִּי כְּמֵת מִלֵּב הָיִיתִי
כִּכְלִי אֹבֵד׃ 14 כִּי שָׁמַעְתִּי ׀
דִּבַּת רַבִּים מָגוֹר מִסָּבִיב
בְּהִוָּסְדָם יַחַד עָלַי לָקַחַת נַפְשִׁי
זָמָמוּ׃ 15 וַאֲנִי ׀ עָלֶיךָ בָטַחְתִּי
יְהוָה אָמַרְתִּי אֱלֹהַי אָתָּה׃ 16
בְּיָדְךָ עִתֹּתָי הַצִּילֵנִי מִיַּד־
אוֹיְבַי וּמֵרֹדְפָי׃ 17 הָאִירָה
פָנֶיךָ עַל־עַבְדֶּךָ הוֹשִׁיעֵנִי
בְחַסְדֶּךָ׃ 18 יְהוָה אַל־אֵבוֹשָׁה
כִּי קְרָאתִיךָ יֵבֹשׁוּ רְשָׁעִים יִדְּמוּ
לִשְׁאוֹל׃ 19 תֵּאָלַמְנָה שִׂפְתֵי
שָׁקֶר הַדֹּבְרוֹת עַל־צַדִּיק עָתָק
בְּגַאֲוָה וָבוּז׃ 20 מָה רַב־טוּבְךָ
אֲשֶׁר־צָפַנְתָּ לִּירֵאֶיךָ פָּעַלְתָּ
לַחֹסִים בָּךְ נֶגֶד בְּנֵי אָדָם׃ 21
תַּסְתִּירֵם ׀ בְּסֵתֶר פָּנֶיךָ מֵרֻכְסֵי
אִישׁ תִּצְפְּנֵם בְּסֻכָּה מֵרִיב
לְשֹׁנוֹת׃ 22 בָּרוּךְ יְהוָה כִּי

17 Let me not be ᵃput to shame, O LORD, for I call upon You;
Let the ᵇwicked be put to shame, let them ᶜbe silent in [1]Sheol.
18 Let the ᵃlying lips be mute,
Which ᵇspeak arrogantly against the righteous
With pride and contempt.

Psa. 31:19 How great is Your ᵃgoodness,
Which You have stored up for those who fear You,
Which You have wrought for those who ᵇtake refuge in You,
Before the sons of men!
20 You hide them in the ᵃsecret place of Your presence from the ᵇconspiracies of man;
You keep them secretly in a [1]shelter from the ᶜstrife of tongues.
21 ᵃBlessed be the LORD,
For He has made ᵇmarvelous His lovingkindness to me in a besieged ᶜcity.
22 As for me, ᵃI said in my alarm,
"I am ᵇcut off from before Your eyes";
Nevertheless You ᶜheard the voice of my supplications
When I cried to You.

Psa. 31:23 O love the LORD, all you ᵃHis godly ones!
The LORD ᵇpreserves the faithful
And fully ᶜrecompenses the proud doer.
24 ᵃBe strong and let your heart take courage,
All you who [1]hope in the LORD.

הַפְלִיא חַסְדֹּו לִי בְּעִיר מָצֹור׃

23 וַאֲנִי ׀ אָמַרְתִּי בְחָפְזִי נִגְרַזְתִּי מִנֶּגֶד עֵינֶיךָ אָכֵן שָׁמַעְתָּ קֹול תַּחֲנוּנַי בְּשַׁוְּעִי אֵלֶיךָ׃ 24 אֶהֱבוּ אֶת־יְהוָה כָּל־חֲסִידָיו אֱמוּנִים נֹצֵר יְהוָה וּמְשַׁלֵּם עַל־יֶתֶר עֹשֵׂה גַאֲוָה׃ 25 חִזְקוּ וְיַאֲמֵץ לְבַבְכֶם כָּל־הַמְיַחֲלִים לַיהוָה׃

References

<table>
<tr><td valign="top">

Psalm 31:1
[a]Ps 31:1-3; 71:1-3
[b]Ps 25:2
[c]Ps 143:1

Psalm 31:2
[1]Or *refuge, protection*
[a]Ps 17:6; 71:2; 86:1; 102:2
[b]Ps 18:2; 71:3

Psalm 31:3
[1]Or *crag*
[a]Ps 18:2
[b]Ps 23:3; 25:11

Psalm 31:4
[a]Ps 25:15
[b]Ps 46:1

Psalm 31:5
[1]Or *faithfulness*
[a]Luke 23:46; Acts 7:59
[b]Ps 55:18; 71:23
[c]Deut 32:4; Ps 71:22

Psalm 31:6
[1]Lit *empty vanities*
[a]Jon 2:8
[b]Ps 52:8

Psalm 31:7
[a]Ps 90:14
[b]Ps 10:14

Psalm 31:8
[a]Deut 32:30; Ps 37:33

</td><td valign="top">

Psalm 31:9
[a]Ps 66:14; 69:17
[b]Ps 6:7
[c]Ps 63:1

Psalm 31:10
[1]Or *bones, substance*
[a]Ps 13:2
[b]Ps 39:11
[c]Ps 32:3; 38:3; 102:3

Psalm 31:11
[a]Ps 69:19
[b]Job 19:13; Ps 38:11; 88:8, 18

Psalm 31:12
[a]Ps 88:5

Psalm 31:13
[1]Lit *whispering*
[a]Ps 50:20; Jer 20:10
[b]Lam 2:22
[c]Ps 62:4; Matt 27:1
[d]Ps 41:7

Psalm 31:14
[a]Ps 140:6

Psalm 31:15
[a]Job 14:5; 24:1
[b]Ps 143:9

Psalm 31:16
[a]Num 6:25; Ps 4:6; 80:3
[b]Ps 6:4

</td></tr>
</table>

Psalm 31:17
[1]I.e. the nether world
[a]Ps 25:2, 20
[b]Ps 25:3
[c]1 Sam 2:9; Ps 94:17; 115:17

Psalm 31:18
[a]Ps 109:2; 120:2
[b]1 Sam 2:3; Ps 94:4; Jude 15

Psalm 31:19
[a]Ps 65:4; 145:7; Is 64:4; Rom 2:4; 11:22
[b]Ps 5:11
[c]Ps 23:5

Psalm 31:20
[1]Or *pavilion*
[a]Ps 27:5
[b]Ps 37:12
[c]Job 5:21; Ps 31:13

Psalm 31:21
[a]Ps 28:6
[b]Ps 17:7
[c]1 Sam 23:7; Ps 87:5

Psalm 31:22
[a]Ps 116:11
[b]Ps 88:5; Is 38:11, 12; Lam 3:54
[c]Ps 18:6; 66:19; 145:19

Psalm 31:23
[a]Ps 30:4; 37:28; 50:5
[b]Ps 145:20; Rev 2:10
[c]Deut 32:41; Ps 94:2

Psalm 31:24
[1]Or *wait for*
[a]Ps 27:14

Targum

Psa. 31:1 For praise; a psalm of David. [2] In your word, O LORD, I have placed my hope; I will never be disappointed; by your generosity save me. [3] Incline your ear to me, in haste save me. Be for me a strong fortress, a fortified stronghold to redeem me. [4] For you are my strength and trust; and for the sake of your name, guide me and sustain me. [5] Take me out of this net that they spread for me, for you are my strength. [6] Into your hand I will place my spirit; you have redeemed me, O LORD, true God. [7] I hate those who observe practices that are like vanity and lies; but I have relied on the LORD. [8] I will rejoice and be glad in your kindness, for you have seen my affliction, you know the troubles of my soul. [9] And you have not handed me over to the hand of my enemy; you have made my feet stand in a broad place. [10] Have mercy on me, O LORD, for I am in distress. My eye is wasted from agitation; my soul and my belly are destroyed. [11] For my life is ended in misery, and my years in sighing; my strength has failed because of my sin, and my limbs are used up. [12] I have become a more shameful thing than all my oppressors, and more so to my neighbors – a fearful thing to those who know me, those who see me in the street flee from my presence. [13] I am forgotten like a dead man from the mind; I have become like a broken vessel of the potter. [14] Because I have heard an evil report which many peoples say about me; terror is all around when they gather together against me; they have planned to take my soul. [15] But I have put my trust in you, O LORD; I said, "You are my God." [16] In your hand are the times of my redemption; save me from the hand of my enemies and persecutors. [17] Shine your countenance on your servant; redeem me by your goodness. [18] O LORD, I will not be disappointed, for I have called upon you; let the wicked be disappointed, let them be silent and descend to Sheol. [19] Let the lips of falsehood be stopped up, [the lips] that speak slander against the righteous in pride and contempt. [20] How great is your goodness that you have hidden for those that fear you; you have acted for those who hope in you, to pay them a good reward in front of the sons of men. [21] You will hide them in a hiding place in the time of your anger from troops of warriors; you will conceal them as in a shelter from the strife of tongues. [22] Blessed be the LORD, for he has exhibited his kindness to me in the walled city. [23] And I thought when I sought to flee, I have been eliminated from the presence of your glory; [but] in truth you heard the sound of my prayer when I made supplication to you. [24] Love the LORD, all his devotees; the LORD keeps the faithful from harm, and pays back the haughty who act proudly. [25] Be strong, and let your mind be sturdy, all you who have confidence in the word of the LORD.

Spiritual Awareness

A spiritual rewrite was not done for this Psalm due to the spiritual nature of the original writing.

Introduction

This Psalm can be best understood by recalling the suffering of the nation of Israel in general and David in particular.

Verse one

King David offered this Psalm to his chief musician. He starts by stating that his full trust is in the LORD. He asks the LORD to help him so that no one may ever deceive him. His ultimate journey is to be in the LORD's righteousness.

Verse two

David's circumstance was dire, and he desperately needed the LORD's protection. We are reminded that barriers on all sides surround us. These barriers offer us protection, and it is within these bounds that the LORD gives us a pleasant home.

Verse three

This verse is an example of parallelism. Verse two and three say the same thing in different ways.

Verse four

David felt assured that the LORD would lead him out the snare of danger that he got himself into.

Verse five

David committed himself to whatever the LORD wanted to happen. By doing so, he knew that the evil forces that were trying to ensnare him would not succeed. He was grateful to the LORD for allowing him to be a part of Israel's history.

Verse six

King David repeats his love for the LORD and dislikes for people who worship idols.

Verse seven and eight

David said that he would only be glad when deliverance and salvation come only from the LORD. He recognizes that the LORD is the only one who can genuinely provide these things.

Verse nine

חָנֵּנִי *(chaneanee)* – means "gracious." As a rule, this word implies a plea for spiritual strength. David asked the LORD to grant him the spiritual strength to solve the problems in his life. By this strength, he would be able to continue his work for the LORD.

Verse ten

There is nothing to add to this verse.

Verse eleven

David said that because so many men had risen against him, the rest of the world had doubts about his character and moral worth. People had become ashamed to know him and would not have anything to do with him.

Verse twelve

There is nothing to add to this verse.

Verse thirteen

Simply put, David's enemies wanted him dead.

Verse fourteen

There is nothing to add to this verse.

Verse fifteen

In this verse, David said that the LORD saved him many times from his enemies. He was confident that the LORD would save him once more.

Verse sixteen

There is nothing to add to this verse

Verse seventeen

There was no reason for David to expect any disappointment from the LORD because he constantly worshiped Him.

Verse eighteen

With this verse, David ends the description of the suffering, which made him feel forsaken. David turns his complete trust to the LORD for help amid trouble. He rectifies the complaint which he had made earlier in the Psalm. The lips that speak injustice in pride and contempt against a righteous man because they see him must stop.

Verse nineteen

David moved from decrying the wicked to extolling the righteous and the salvation destined for them.

Verse twenty

David asked the LORD to take the wicked people trying to kill him and hide them away so they could not be seen. This means that he is asking the LORD to rid him of these enemies. Since the LORD anointed David, it is logical to ask the LORD to remove his enemies from the Earth. Forming the nation of Israel was easier when enemies were removed.

Verse twenty-one

The verse refers to a fortified city. The only way to take such a city in David's time was through a siege.

Verse twenty-two

There is nothing to add to this verse.

Verse twenty-three

Even when David could not feel the LORD, he knew that the Shekinah was there.

Verse twenty-four

David concludes the Psalm with this statement. It is sound advice and a summation of the Psalm.

Psalm 32

New American Standard 1995	Hebrew

Psa. 32:0 *A Psalm* of David. A †Maskil.

Psa. 32:1 [a]How blessed is he whose transgression is forgiven,
  Whose sin is covered!
2 How blessed is the man to whom the LORD [a]does not impute iniquity,
  And in whose spirit there is [b]no deceit!

Psa. 32:3 When [a]I kept silent *about my sin,* [b]my [1]body wasted away
  Through my [2c]groaning all day long.
4 For day and night [a]Your hand was heavy upon me;
  My [1b]vitality was drained away *as* with the fever heat of summer. [2]Selah.
5 I [a]acknowledged my sin to You,
  And my iniquity I [b]did not hide;
  I said, "I will confess my transgressions to the LORD";
  And You [d]forgave the [1]guilt of my sin. Selah.
6 Therefore, let everyone who is godly pray to You [1a]in a time when You may be found;
  Surely [b]in a flood of great waters they will not reach him.
7 You are [a]my hiding place; You [b]preserve me from trouble;
  You surround me with [1c]songs of deliverance. Selah.

לְדָוִד מַשְׂכִּיל אַשְׁרֵי **Psa. 32:1**

נְשׂוּי־פֶּשַׁע כְּסוּי חֲטָאָה: 2

אַשְׁרֵי אָדָם לֹא יַחְשֹׁב יְהוָה לוֹ

עָוֹן וְאֵין בְּרוּחוֹ רְמִיָּה: 3 כִּי־

הֶחֱרַשְׁתִּי בָּלוּ עֲצָמָי בְּשַׁאֲגָתִי

כָּל־הַיּוֹם: 4 כִּי יוֹמָם וָלַיְלָה

תִּכְבַּד עָלַי יָדֶךָ נֶהְפַּךְ לְשַׁדִּי

בְּחַרְבֹנֵי קַיִץ סֶלָה: 5 חַטָּאתִי

אוֹדִיעֲךָ וַעֲוֹנִי לֹא־כִסִּיתִי

אָמַרְתִּי אוֹדֶה עֲלֵי פְשָׁעַי

לַיהוָה וְאַתָּה נָשָׂאתָ עֲוֹן

חַטָּאתִי סֶלָה: 6 עַל־זֹאת

יִתְפַּלֵּל כָּל־חָסִיד אֵלֶיךָ לְעֵת

מְצֹא רַק לְשֵׁטֶף מַיִם רַבִּים

אֵלָיו לֹא יַגִּיעוּ: 7 אַתָּה סֵתֶר

לִי מִצַּר תִּצְּרֵנִי רָנֵּי פַלֵּט

תְּסוֹבְבֵנִי סֶלָה: 8 אַשְׂכִּילְךָ

וְאוֹרְךָ בְּדֶרֶךְ־זוּ תֵלֵךְ אִיעֲצָה

עָלֶיךָ עֵינִי: 9 אַל־תִּהְיוּ כְּסוּס

כְּפֶרֶד אֵין הָבִין בְּמֶתֶג־וָרֶסֶן

עֶדְיוֹ לִבְלוֹם בַּל קְרֹב אֵלֶיךָ:

Psa. 32:8   I will [a]instruct you and teach you in the way which you should go;

    I will counsel you [b]with My eye upon you.

9   Do not be [a]as the horse or as the mule which have no understanding,

    Whose trappings include bit and bridle to hold them in check,

    Otherwise they will not come near to you.

10   Many are the [a]sorrows of the wicked,

    But [b]he who trusts in the LORD, lovingkindness shall surround him.

11   Be [a]glad in the LORD and rejoice, you righteous ones;

    And shout for joy, all you who are [b]upright in heart.

רַבִּים מַכְאוֹבִים לָרָשָׁע 10
וְהַבּוֹטֵחַ בַּיהוָה חֶסֶד יְסוֹבְבֶנּוּ :
שִׂמְחוּ בַיהוָה וְגִילוּ צַדִּיקִים 11
וְהַרְנִינוּ כָּל־יִשְׁרֵי־לֵב :

References

Psalm 32:0
¹Possibly *Contemplative,* or *Didactic,* or *Skillful Psalm*

Psalm 32:1
ᵃPs 85:2; 103:3; Rom 4:7, 8

Psalm 32:2
ᵃ2 Cor 5:19
ᵇJohn 1:47

Psalm 32:3
¹Or *bones, substance*
²Lit *roaring*
ᵃPs 39:2, 3
ᵇPs 31:10
ᶜPs 38:8

Psalm 32:4
¹Lit *life juices were turned into the drought of summer*
²*Selah* may mean: *Pause, Crescendo* or *Musical interlude*
ᵃ1 Sam 5:6; Job 23:2; 33:7; Ps 38:2; 39:10
ᵇPs 22:15

Psalm 32:5
¹Or *iniquity*
ᵃLev 26:40
ᵇJob 31:33
ᶜPs 38:18; Prov 28:13; 1 John 1:9
ᵈPs 103:12

Psalm 32:6
¹Lit *in a time of finding out*
ᵃPs 69:13; Is 55:6
ᵇPs 46:1-3; 69:1; 124:5; 144:7; Is 43:2

Psalm 32:7
¹Or *shouts*
ᵃPs 9:9; 31:20; 91:1; 119:114
ᵇPs 121:7
ᶜEx 15:1; Judg 5:1; Ps 40:3

Psalm 32:8
ᵃPs 25:8
ᵇPs 33:18

Psalm 32:9
ᵃProv 26:3

Psalm 32:10
ᵃPs 16:4; Prov 13:21; Rom 2:9
ᵇPs 5:11, 12; Prov 16:20

Psalm 32:11
ᵃPs 64:10; 68:3; 97:12
ᵇPs 7:10; 64:10

Targum

Psa. 32:1 Of David. Good counsel. David said, "How blessed is the one whose impieties they forgive, whose sins they cover over." [2] How happy was Moses, son of Amram, to whom the LORD did not reckon his sins, because there was no guile in his spirit. [3] Because I have been silent from the words of Torah, my bones waste away while I groan all day. [4] Because day and night your punishment is severe upon me, my moisture is turned to, as it were, the hot wind of summer forever. [5] My sin I will tell you and my iniquity I have not covered. I said, "I will confess my rebellions in the presence of the LORD"; and you forgave the iniquity of my sin forever. [6] Because of this let every pious man pray in your presence at the time of his favor; indeed, at the time when many Gentiles come like waters, to him they will not come near to do harm. [7] You are the LORD; hide me, from the oppressor guard me; the joy of salvation will surround me forever. [8] I will enlighten you and teach you; in this way you shall go; I will advise you and put my eye upon you for good. [9] Do not be like a horse or mule who have no intelligence; both muzzle and halter are its trappings to be kept silent; let it not come near you. [10] Many are the pains of the wicked; but favor will surround the one who trusts in the LORD. [11] Rejoice in the word of the LORD, and be glad, O righteous; and give praise, all you with upright hearts.

Spiritual Awareness

The spiritual rewrite for the verses is in bold.

Introduction

This is the first Psalm of David that addresses repentance. David explains that repentance is more than simply attaining Divine forgiveness. All types of repentance bring about at least some forgiveness. The soul cannot be returned to its state before a sin was created unless the heart is cleansed and the spirit is properly conditioned. The highest level of purity and forgiveness is achieved on Yom Kippur (Leviticus 16:30).

Superscript

מַשְׂכִּיל (mas'ceel) – means "poem." The psalms that have this word in their superscript contain an instructive lecture or explanation.

A Maskil by David

Verse one

אַשְׁרֵי נְשׂוּי (ash'rai n'soo) – means "blessed forgiven." When these two words are combined in verse, it means "raised above and tested against transgression." Happy is the person who is tried against transgressions and is protected from sin. Our own moral energy is adequate to help us to remain free from transgressions.

Verse seven

You are a shade to me even then, You preserve me from distress, You cause the rejoicing of deliverance to encompass me. Meditate on this verse.

Verse eight

אַשְׂכִּילְךָ (as'keel'cha) – literally it means "I shall permit you to employ your mind for intelligent perception and reasoning. In other words, I shall cause you to engage in rational contemplation.

I shall instruct you and teach you how you are to go; I would advise you from my own experience.

Verse nine

The Psalmist implores us not to be like dumb animals. People are always to show that they are a human beings with intelligence gifted to us by the LORD.

Don't be like a horse or mule that is devoid of intelligence. It is their mark that must be restrained by the bit or bridle so that they will not come near to you.

Verse ten

There are sufferings in the world that are intended solely for people who will not submit to the authority of the LORD's Law. People who sin and seek forgiveness from the LORD through repentance will be sheltered by His love.

Many sufferings are intended only for the lawless who don't follow the LORD's Law, but as for persons who trust in the LORD, the LORD will surround that person with mercy.

Verse eleven

All people who place their faith and trust in the LORD will rejoice and shout for joy.

Therefore, be glad in the LORD, and rejoice with great joy for all who are righteous, and let those who are upright in heart be of good cheer.

Complete Psalm Rewrite Emphasizing Spiritual Awareness

A Maskil by David

Happy is the person who is tried against transgression and protected from sin.

Happy is the person in whom the LORD sees no iniquity and in whose spirit there is no deceit.

For when I kept silent, my bones wore away through my groaning all day long.

For day and night, Your hand lay heavily upon me; my marrow was turned as in the droughts of the heat of summer. Meditate on this verse.

LORD, you had already removed the iniquity of my sin before I admitted it to you. Meditate on this verse.

Therefore, let every one of devotion seek clarity of judgment before You at the time of affliction. The mighty flood of great waters will not reach him to wash away sins.

You are a shade to me even then, You preserve me from distress, You cause the rejoicing of deliverance to encompass me. Meditate on this verse.

I shall instruct you and teach you how you are to go; I would advise you from my own experience.

Don't be like a horse or mule that is devoid of intelligence. It is their mark that must be restrained by the bit or bridle so that they will not come near to you.

Many sufferings are intended only for the lawless who don't follow the LORD's Law, but as for persons who trust in the LORD, the LORD will surround that person with mercy.

Therefore, be glad in the LORD, and rejoice with great joy for all who are righteous, and let those who are upright in heart be of good cheer.

Psalm 33

New American Standard 1995	Hebrew
Psa. 33:1 Sing for joy in the LORD, O you righteous ones; Praise is ^bbecoming to the upright. 2 Give thanks to the LORD with the ^dlyre; Sing praises to Him with a ^bharp of ten strings. 3 Sing to Him a ^anew song; Play skillfully with ^ba shout of joy. 4 For the word of the LORD ^ais upright, And all His work is *done* ^bin faithfulness. 5 He ^aloves righteousness and justice; The ^bearth is full of the lovingkindness of the LORD. **Psa. 33:6** By the ^aword of the LORD the heavens were made, And ^bby the breath of His mouth ^call their host. 7 He gathers the ^awaters of the sea together ¹as a heap; He lays up the deeps in storehouses. 8 Let ^aall the Earth fear the LORD; Let all the inhabitants of the world ^bstand in awe of Him. 9 For ^aHe spoke, and it was done; He commanded, and it ¹stood fast. 10 The LORD ^anullifies the counsel of the nations;	רַנְּנ֥וּ צַדִּיקִים֮ בַּֽיהוָ֫ה Psa. 33:1 ‏לַ֭יְשָׁרִים נָאוָ֣ה תְהִלָּֽה׃ ‏² הוֹד֣וּ לַיהוָ֣ה בְּכִנּ֑וֹר בְּנֵ֥בֶל עָ֝שׂ֗וֹר ‏זַמְּרוּ־לֽוֹ׃ ³ שִֽׁירוּ־ל֖וֹ שִׁ֣יר חָדָ֑שׁ ‏הֵיטִ֥יבוּ נַ֝גֵּ֗ן בִּתְרוּעָֽה׃ ⁴ כִּֽי־יָשָׁ֥ר ‏דְּבַר־יְהוָ֑ה וְכָל־מַ֝עֲשֵׂ֗הוּ בֶּאֱמוּנָֽה׃ ⁵ אֹ֭הֵב צְדָקָ֣ה וּמִשְׁפָּ֑ט חֶ֥סֶד יְ֝הוָ֗ה מָלְאָ֥ה הָאָֽרֶץ׃ ⁶ בִּדְבַ֣ר יְ֭הוָה שָׁמַ֣יִם נַעֲשׂ֑וּ וּבְר֥וּחַ פִּ֝֗יו כָּל־צְבָאָֽם׃ ⁷ כֹּנֵ֣ס כַּ֭נֵּד מֵ֣י הַיָּ֑ם נֹתֵ֖ן בְּאֹצָר֣וֹת תְּהוֹמֽוֹת׃ ⁸ יִֽירְא֣וּ מֵ֭יְהוָה כָּל־הָאָ֑רֶץ מִמֶּ֥נּוּ יָ֝ג֗וּרוּ כָּל־יֹשְׁבֵ֥י תֵבֵֽל׃ ⁹ כִּ֤י ה֣וּא אָמַ֣ר וַיֶּ֑הִי הֽוּא־צִ֝וָּ֗ה וַֽיַּעֲמֹֽד׃ ¹⁰ יְֽהוָ֗ה הֵפִ֥יר עֲצַת־גּוֹיִ֑ם הֵ֝נִ֗יא מַחְשְׁב֥וֹת עַמִּֽים׃ ¹¹ עֲצַ֣ת יְ֭הוָה לְעוֹלָ֣ם תַּעֲמֹ֑ד מַחְשְׁב֥וֹת לִ֝בּ֗וֹ לְדֹ֣ר וָדֹֽר׃ ¹² אַשְׁרֵ֣י הַ֭גּוֹי אֲשֶׁר־יְהוָ֣ה אֱלֹהָ֑יו הָעָ֓ם ׀ בָּחַ֖ר לְנַחֲלָ֣ה לֽוֹ׃ ¹³ מִ֭שָּׁמַיִם הִבִּ֣יט יְהוָ֑ה רָ֝אָ֗ה אֶֽת־כָּל־בְּנֵ֥י הָאָדָֽם׃ ¹⁴ מִֽמְּכוֹן־

He frustrates the plans of the peoples.

11 The ᵃcounsel of the LORD stands forever,

The ᵇplans of His heart from generation to generation.

12 Blessed is the ᶜnation whose God is the LORD,

The people whom He has ᵇchosen for His own inheritance.

Psa. 33:13 The LORD ᵈlooks from heaven;

He ᵇsees all the sons of men;

14 From ᵈHis dwelling place He looks out

On all the inhabitants of the Earth,

15 He who ᵃfashions ¹the hearts of them all,

He who ᵇunderstands all their works.

16 ᵈThe king is not saved by a mighty army;

A warrior is not delivered by great strength.

17 A ᵃhorse is a false hope for victory;

Nor does it deliver anyone by its great strength.

Psa. 33:18 Behold, ᵃthe eye of the LORD is on those who fear Him,

On those who ᵇhope for His lovingkindness,

19 To ᵃdeliver their soul from death

And to keep them alive ᵇin famine.

20 Our soul ᵃwaits for the LORD;

He is our ᵇhelp and our shield.

21 For our ᵃheart rejoices in Him,

Because we trust in His holy name.

22 Let Your lovingkindness, O LORD, be upon us,

שֻׁבְתּוֹ הִשְׁגִּיחַ אֶל כָּל־יֹשְׁבֵי הָאָרֶץ: 15 הַיֹּצֵר יַחַד לִבָּם הַמֵּבִין אֶל־כָּל־מַעֲשֵׂיהֶם: 16 אֵין־הַמֶּלֶךְ נוֹשָׁע בְּרָב־חָיִל גִּבּוֹר לֹא־יִנָּצֵל בְּרָב־כֹּחַ: 17 שֶׁקֶר הַסּוּס לִתְשׁוּעָה וּבְרֹב חֵילוֹ לֹא יְמַלֵּט: 18 הִנֵּה עֵין יְהוָה אֶל־יְרֵאָיו לַמְיַחֲלִים לְחַסְדּוֹ: 19 לְהַצִּיל מִמָּוֶת נַפְשָׁם וּלְחַיּוֹתָם בָּרָעָב: 20 נַפְשֵׁנוּ חִכְּתָה לַיהוָה עֶזְרֵנוּ וּמָגִנֵּנוּ הוּא: 21 כִּי־בוֹ יִשְׂמַח לִבֵּנוּ כִּי בְשֵׁם קָדְשׁוֹ בָטָחְנוּ: 22 יְהִי־חַסְדְּךָ יְהוָה עָלֵינוּ כַּאֲשֶׁר יִחַלְנוּ לָךְ:

According as we have [1]hoped in You.	

References

<table>
<tr><td valign="top">

Psalm 33:1
[a]Ps 32:11; Phil 3:1; 4:4
[b]Ps 92:1; 147:1

Psalm 33:2
[a]Ps 71:22; 147:7
[b]Ps 144:9

Psalm 33:3
[a]Ps 40:3; 96:1; 98:1; 144:9; Is 42:10; Rev 5:9
[b]Ps 98:4

Psalm 33:4
[a]Ps 19:8
[b]Ps 119:90

Psalm 33:5
[a]Ps 11:7; 37:28
[b]Ps 119:64

Psalm 33:6
[a]Gen 1:6; Ps 148:5; Heb 11:3
[b]Ps 104:30
[c]Gen 2:1

Psalm 33:7
[1]Some versions read *in a water skin*; i.e. container
[a]Ex 15:8; Josh 3:16; Ps 78:13

Psalm 33:8
[a]Ps 67:7
[b]Ps 96:9

Psalm 33:9
[1]Or *stood forth*
[a]Gen 1:3; Ps 148:5

</td><td valign="top">

Psalm 33:10
[a]Ps 2:1-3; Is 8:10; 19:3

Psalm 33:11
[a]Job 23:12; Prov 19:21
[b]Ps 40:5; 92:5; 139:17; Is 55:8

Psalm 33:12
[a]Ps 144:15
[b]Ex 19:5; Deut 7:6; Ps 28:9

Psalm 33:13
[a]Job 28:24; Ps 14:2
[b]Ps 11:4

Psalm 33:14
[a]1 Kin 8:39, 43; Ps 102:19

Psalm 33:15
[1]Or *their heart together*
[a]Job 10:8; Ps 119:73
[b]2 Chr 16:9; Job 34:21; Jer 32:19

Psalm 33:16
[a]Ps 44:6; 60:11

Psalm 33:17
[a]Ps 20:7; 147:10; Prov 21:31

Psalm 33:18
[1]Or *wait*
[a]Job 36:7; Ps 32:8; 34:15; 1 Pet 3:12
[b]Ps 32:10; 147:11

Psalm 33:19
[a]Ps 56:13; Acts 12:11
[b]Job 5:20; Ps 37:19

</td></tr>
</table>

Psalm 33:20
[a]Ps 62:1; 130:6; Is 8:17
[b]Ps 115:9

Psalm 33:21
[a]Ps 13:5; 28:7; Zech 10:7; John 16:22

Psalm 33:22
[1]Or *waited for*

Targum

Psa. 33:1 Give praise, O righteous, in the presence of the LORD; praise is seemly for the upright. [2] Give thanks in the presence of the LORD with the lyre; with the harp of ten strings give him praise. [3] Give praise in the presence of the LORD with a new song; praise well with a shout. [4] For the word of the LORD is right, and all his deeds are reliable. [5] He loves righteousness and justice; the goodness of the LORD fills the Earth. [6] By the word of the LORD were the heavens made; and by the breath of his mouth, all their armies. [7] Who gathers as in a bottle the waters of the sea; he puts them in the treasuries of the deeps. [8] In the presence of the LORD all who dwell on the Earth will be afraid; all the inhabitants of the world will tremble because of him. [9] Because he says it, and it is; he commanded, and it took place. [10] The LORD shattered the counsel of the Gentiles, frustrated the plans of the nations. [11] The counsel of the LORD stands forever, the thoughts of his heart for all generations. [12] Happy is the man whose god is the LORD, the people that he chose for his inheritance. [13] From heaven the LORD looked, he saw all the sons of men. [14] From the residence of his dwelling he looked out at all the inhabitants of the Earth. [15] Who created them, forming their heart together, and discerning all their deeds. [16] The king is not redeemed by the abundance of his forces; the warrior is not saved by the abundance of his strength. [17] The horse is deceitful for redemption; and by the abundance of its strength one is not saved. [18] Behold, the eye of the LORD sees those who fear him, those who hope for his kindness. [19] To save their soul from death, and to keep them alive in famine. [20] Our soul looks for the redemption of the LORD; he is our help and shield. [21] For our heart will rejoice in his word, because in his holy name we have placed our trust. [22] May your goodness be upon us, O LORD, as we have put our hopes in you.

Spiritual Awareness

The spiritual rewrite for the verses are in bold.

Verse 1

The Sage Malbim believed that this Psalm says that the LORD controls the world in two different ways. The first way is through the Laws of Nature, which are pre-ordained and unchanging. The second way is through *hashgachah*. This word means the personal supervision and intervention of the LORD. How the LORD participates in the affairs of humans depends on human deeds for better or for worse.

The Laws of Nature served to conceal the LORD's supervision. All people who genuinely seek to understand this revelation will be elevated. The wicked will become good, and the goodwill will become better.

O righteous people exult the LORD; it is appropriate for the upright to sing praises so that the LORD may reveal His might.

Verse 2

Human speech is inadequate alone to praise the LORD; therefore, the sound of the harp and lyre is necessary.

Render thanks to the LORD with the harp and sing praises to Him with the psaltery.

Verse 3

שִׁירוּ־לוֹ (sheroo-lo) – means "sing to." The primary usage of this phrase is to denote "singing praises." The psalmist tells us to sing praises to the invisible hand of the LORD, which is a part of all human history. The difference between verses one and two is in this verse is that the psalmist tells us to sing a new song.

Sing Him a new song, express it intones as it is seemly, with deep inner emotion.

Verse 4

This verse is the theme of the hymn proclaiming the praise of the LORD so that man might come to know and understand Him.

For the word of the LORD is for the upright, and His work is done in faithfulness.

Verse five

The Earth is full of the life-giving love of the LORD. He showers us with blessings. His merciful love fills the Earth. He loves justice as well as righteousness. The LORD requires humanity to be just and loyal to the LORD.

Chesed fills the world with lovingkindness of the LORD, for the LORD loves righteousness and justice.

Verse six

The Heavens were made so that humanity might reach that moral goal of Divine sovereignty which is indicated by the tetragrammaton name of the LORD.

By the word of the LORD, the Heavens were created, and all the hosts were created by His word.

Verse Seven

כֹּנֵס כַּנֵּד (konas kanaid) – means "gathers heap." This construction is used in the Torah to refer to the parting of the Sea of Reeds (Red Sea). This miracle of the LORD occurred outside of the framework of the "laws of nature." These occasional miracles help humans understand that even the natural and everyday order of things is the work of the LORD. This Psalm calls attention to the parting of the Sea of Reeds as the most significant of all the acts that demonstrated the LORD's rule and supremacy.

He who gathers the sea's waters like a wall also stores up floods in treasure chambers.

Verse 8

Every human living on the Earth should know that the very ground they are standing on is because the LORD desired to create it.

Therefore, let all the Earth show the LORD reverence; let all the world inhabitants stand back in awe of Him.

Verse 9

The LORD speaks His commandments, and they are fulfilled.

For He spoke, and it was; He also commanded, and it stood still.

Verse 10

מַחְשְׁבוֹת עַמִּים (mach'sheevot ameem) – means "peoples' plans." These plans are the thoughts that motivate the acts of humans against one another in their domestic relationships.

The LORD has brought to naught the counsel of the people.

Verse 11

The plans that nations have cherished throughout history, the quest for power, face opposition by the plans of the LORD, which is to establish the kingdom of peace under the supreme sovereignty of love and righteousness.

The counsel of the LORD stands for the people; the thought of His heart shall be the heritage of all generations.

Verse 12

Any nation of the world who believes in the LORD will be blessed.

Blessed is the nation whose God is the LORD, for they will receive His inheritance.

Verse 13

The LORD looked down from Heaven one day and beheld all the sons of man.

Verse 14

This verse is a parallel verse to verse 13.

The LORD looked out on the inhabitants of the Earth from his dwelling place.

Verse 15

The LORD looks upon humans and measures the worth of their deeds by the criteria He established for their creation. The LORD intended for humans to live together and to support each other.

He who fashions their hearts for one another; Who considers all their doing

Verse 16 & 17

The LORD saw the unfettered reign of selfish violence and tyranny as a supreme human goal. Gevurah will judge kings and heroes.

A king is not saved by a mighty army, nor is a hero delivered by his strength.

A horse is a vain hope for victory, nor can it escape by its great strength.

Verse 18

The LORD watches human actions to see if these actions are guided solely by His commandments. Those who call upon Chesed will receive the love of the LORD.

Behold the eye of the LORD is toward all who revere Him, and they hope for Chesed to shine upon them.

Verse 19

Parts of this Psalm relate to the time of Israel's departure from Egypt. In this verse, the psalmist talks about the LORD's deliverance from physical and national annihilation in Egypt. The LORD fed His people with manna from Heaven.

To deliver their souls from death and to keep them alive in famine.

Verse 20

It was our soul that waited for the LORD; He is still our help and our shield.

Verse 21

We should place our trust and faith in the LORD.

For it is only in the LORD that our heart rejoices because we have put our trust in His Holy name.

Verse 22

May Chesed be upon us LORD, we have waited for you.

Complete Psalm Rewrite Emphasizing Spiritual Awareness

O righteous people exult the LORD; it is appropriate for the upright to sing praises so that the LORD may reveal His might.

Render thanks to the LORD with the harp and sing praises to Him with the psaltery.

Sing Him a new song, express it intones as it is seemly, with deep inner emotion.

For the word of the LORD is for the upright, and His work is done in faithfulness.

Chesed fills the world with lovingkindness of the LORD, for the LORD loves righteousness and justice.

By the word of the LORD, the Heavens were created, and all the hosts were created by His word.

He who gathers the sea's waters like a wall also stores up floods in treasure chambers.

Therefore, let all the Earth show the LORD reverence; let all the world inhabitants stand back in awe of Him.

For He spoke, and it was; He also commanded, and it stood still.

The LORD has brought to naught the counsel of the people.

The counsel of the LORD stands for the people; the thought of His heart shall be the heritage of all generations.

Blessed is the nation whose God is the LORD, for they will receive His inheritance.

The LORD looked down from Heaven one day and beheld all the sons of man.

The LORD looked out on the inhabitants of the Earth from his dwelling place.

He who fashions their hearts for one another; Who considers all their doing

A king is not saved by a mighty army, nor is a hero delivered by his strength.

A horse is a vain hope for victory, nor can it escape by its great strength.

Behold the eye of the LORD is toward all who revere Him, and they hope for Chesed to shine upon them.

To deliver their souls from death and to keep them alive in famine.

It was our soul that waited for the LORD; He is still our help and our shield.

For it is only in the LORD that our heart rejoices because we have put our trust in His Holy name.

May Chesed be upon us LORD, we have waited for you.

Psalm 34

New American Standard 1995	Hebrew

Psa. 34:0 *A Psalm* of David when he †feigned madness before °Abimelech, who drove him away and he departed.

Psa. 34:1 I will *bless the LORD at all times;
His *praise shall continually be in my mouth.
2 My soul will *make its boast in the LORD;
The *humble will hear it and rejoice.
3 O *magnify the LORD with me,
And let us *exalt His name together.

Psa. 34:4 I *sought the LORD, and He answered me,
And *delivered me from all my fears.
5 They *looked to Him and were radiant,
And their faces will *never be ashamed.
6 This *poor man cried, and *the LORD heard him
And saved him out of all his troubles.
7 The *angel of the LORD encamps around those who fear Him,
And rescues them.

Psa. 34:8 O *taste and see that the LORD is good;
How *blessed is the man who takes refuge in Him!
9 O fear the LORD, you *His saints;
For to those who fear Him there is *no want.
10 The young lions do lack and suffer hunger;
But they who seek the LORD shall *not be in want of any good thing.
11 *Come, you children, listen to me;
*I will teach you *the fear of the LORD.
12 *Who is the man who desires life

Psa. 34:1 לְדָוִד בְּשַׁנּוֹתוֹ אֶת־טַעְמוֹ לִפְנֵי אֲבִימֶלֶךְ וַיְגָרֲשֵׁהוּ וַיֵּלַךְ׃ 2 אֲבָרֲכָה אֶת־יְהוָה בְּכָל־עֵת תָּמִיד תְּהִלָּתוֹ בְּפִי׃ 3 בַּיהוָה תִּתְהַלֵּל נַפְשִׁי יִשְׁמְעוּ עֲנָוִים וְיִשְׂמָחוּ׃ 4 גַּדְּלוּ לַיהוָה אִתִּי וּנְרוֹמְמָה שְׁמוֹ יַחְדָּו׃ 5 דָּרַשְׁתִּי אֶת־יְהוָה וְעָנָנִי וּמִכָּל־מְגוּרוֹתַי הִצִּילָנִי׃ 6 הִבִּיטוּ אֵלָיו וְנָהָרוּ וּפְנֵיהֶם אַל־יֶחְפָּרוּ׃ 7 זֶה עָנִי קָרָא וַיהוָה שָׁמֵעַ וּמִכָּל־צָרוֹתָיו הוֹשִׁיעוֹ׃ 8 חֹנֶה מַלְאַךְ־יְהוָה סָבִיב לִירֵאָיו וַיְחַלְּצֵם׃ 9 טַעֲמוּ וּרְאוּ כִּי־טוֹב יְהוָה אַשְׁרֵי הַגֶּבֶר יֶחֱסֶה־בּוֹ׃ 10 יְראוּ אֶת־יְהוָה קְדֹשָׁיו כִּי־אֵין מַחְסוֹר לִירֵאָיו׃ 11 כְּפִירִים רָשׁוּ וְרָעֵבוּ וְדֹרְשֵׁי יְהוָה לֹא־יַחְסְרוּ כָל־טוֹב׃ 12 לְכוּ־בָנִים שִׁמְעוּ־לִי יִרְאַת

And loves *length of* days that he may *b*see good?
13 Keep *a*your tongue from evil
And your lips from speaking *b*deceit.
14 *a*Depart from evil and do good;
Seek peace and *b*pursue it.

Psa. 34:15 The *a*eyes of the LORD are toward the righteous
And His ears are *open* to their cry.
16 The *a*face of the LORD is against evildoers,
To *b*cut off the memory of them from the earth.
17 *The righteous* *a*cry, and the LORD hears
And delivers them out of all their troubles.
18 The LORD *a*is near to the *b*brokenhearted
And saves those who are *1c*crushed in spirit.

Psa. 34:19 *a*Many are the *b*afflictions of the righteous,
But the LORD *c*delivers him out of them all.
20 He keeps all his bones,
*a*Not one of them is broken.
21 *a*Evil shall slay the wicked,
And those who hate the righteous will be *1*condemned.
22 The LORD *a*redeems the soul of His servants,
And none of those who *b*take refuge in Him will be *1*condemned.

יְהֹוָ֣ה אֲלַמֶּדְכֶֽם׃ 13 מִי־הָאִ֗ישׁ הֶ֭חָפֵץ חַיִּ֑ים אֹהֵ֥ב יָ֝מִ֗ים לִרְא֥וֹת טֽוֹב׃ 14 נְצֹ֣ר לְשׁוֹנְךָ֣ מֵרָ֑ע וּ֝שְׂפָתֶ֗יךָ מִדַּבֵּ֥ר מִרְמָֽה׃ 15 ס֣וּר מֵ֭רָע וַעֲשֵׂה־ט֑וֹב בַּקֵּ֖שׁ שָׁל֣וֹם וְרׇדְפֵֽהוּ׃ 16 עֵינֵ֣י יְ֭הֹוָה אֶל־צַדִּיקִ֑ים וְ֝אׇזְנָ֗יו אֶל־שַׁוְעָתָֽם׃ 17 פְּנֵ֣י יְ֭הֹוָה בְּעֹ֣שֵׂי רָ֑ע לְהַכְרִ֖ית מֵאֶ֣רֶץ זִכְרָֽם׃ 18 צָעֲק֣וּ וַיהֹוָ֣ה שָׁמֵ֑עַ וּמִכׇּל־צָ֝רוֹתָ֗ם הִצִּילָֽם׃ 19 קָר֣וֹב יְ֭הֹוָה לְנִשְׁבְּרֵי־לֵ֑ב וְֽאֶת־דַּכְּאֵי־ר֥וּחַ יוֹשִֽׁיעַ׃ 20 רַ֭בּוֹת רָע֣וֹת צַדִּ֑יק וּ֝מִכֻּלָּ֗ם יַצִּילֶ֥נּוּ יְהֹוָֽה׃ 21 שֹׁמֵ֥ר כׇּל־עַצְמוֹתָ֑יו אַחַ֥ת מֵ֝הֵ֗נָּה לֹ֣א נִשְׁבָּֽרָה׃ 22 תְּמוֹתֵ֣ת רָשָׁ֣ע רָעָ֑ה וְשֹׂנְאֵ֖י צַדִּ֣יק יֶאְשָֽׁמוּ׃ 23 פּוֹדֶ֣ה יְהֹוָה נֶ֣פֶשׁ עֲבָדָ֑יו וְלֹ֥א יֶ֝אְשְׁמ֗וּ כׇּל־הַחֹסִ֥ים בּֽוֹ׃ --

References

Psalm 34:0
¹Or *changed his behavior*
°Possibly a title of King Achish of Gath,
see 1 Sam 21:10-15

Psalm 34:1
ᵃEph 5:20; 1 Thess 5:18
ᵇPs 71:6

Psalm 34:2
ᵃPs 44:8; Jer 9:24; 1 Cor 1:31
ᵇPs 69:32

Psalm 34:3
ᵃPs 35:27; 69:30; Luke 1:46
ᵇPs 18:46

Psalm 34:4
ᵃ2 Chr 15:2; Ps 9:10; Matt 7:7
ᵇPs 34:6, 17, 19

Psalm 34:5
ᵃPs 36:9; Is 60:5
ᵇPs 25:3

Psalm 34:6
¹Or *afflicted*
ᵃPs 34:4

Psalm 34:7
ᵃPs 91:11; Dan 6:22

Psalm 34:8
ᵃPs 119:103; Heb 6:5; 1 Pet 2:3
ᵇPs 2:12

Psalm 34:9
ᵃPs 31:23
ᵇPs 23:1

Psalm 34:10
ᵃPs 84:11

Psalm 34:11
ᵃPs 66:16
ᵇPs 32:8
ᶜPs 111:10

Psalm 34:12
ᵃPs 34:12-16; 1 Pet 3:10-12
ᵇEccl 3:13

Psalm 34:13
ᵃPs 141:3; Prov 13:3; James 1:26
ᵇ1 Pet 2:22

Psalm 34:14
ᵃPs 37:27; Is 1:16, 17
ᵇRom 14:19; Heb 12:14

Psalm 34:15
ᵃJob 36:7; Ps 33:18

Psalm 34:16
ᵃLev 17:10; Jer 44:11; Amos 9:4
ᵇJob 18:17; Ps 9:6; 109:15; Prov 10:7

Psalm 34:17
ᵃPs 34:6; 145:19

Psalm 34:18
[1]Or *contrite*
[a]Ps 145:18
[b]Ps 147:3; Is 61:1
[c]Ps 51:17; Is 57:15

Psalm 34:19
[a]Prov 24:16
[b]Ps 71:20; 2 Tim 3:11f
[c]Ps 34:4, 6, 17

Psalm 34:20
[a]John 19:33, 36

Psalm 34:21
[1]Or *held guilty*
[a]Ps 94:23; 140:11; Prov 24:16

Psalm 34:22
[1]V 21, note 1
[a]1 Kin 1:29; Ps 71:23
[b]Ps 37:40

Targum

Psa. 34:1 Of David, when he disguised his intelligence before Abimelech, who dismissed him, and he left. ² I will bless the LORD at all times, his praise is always in my mouth. ³ My soul makes her boast in the word of the LORD; the humble will hear and rejoice. ⁴ Ascribe greatness in the presence of the LORD with me, and we will exalt his name together. ⁵ I sought instruction from the presence of the LORD and he answered me; and from all my fears he delivered me. ⁶ They looked toward him and received light; and their faces were not dismayed. ⁷ This poor one prayed; in the presence of the LORD it was heard, and he redeemed him from all his troubles. ⁸ The angel of the LORD encamps around those who fear him, and he saved them. ⁹ Recognize and see that the LORD is good; happy the man who has placed his trust in his word. ¹⁰ Have fear in the presence of the LORD, O you his holy ones; for there is nothing lacking to those who fear him. ¹¹ The sons of the lion became poor and were hungry; but those who seek the instruction of the LORD lack no good thing. ¹² Come, children, receive [teaching] from me; I will teach you the fear of the LORD. ¹³ Who is the man who seeks life, loves days in order to see good? ¹⁴ Guard your tongue from evil, and your lips from speaking deceit. ¹⁵ Turn from evil and do good; seek peace and pursue after it. ¹⁶ The eyes of the LORD are toward the righteous; and his ears, to receive their prayer. ¹⁷ The face of the LORD is wrathful against evildoers, to expunge their memory from the earth. ¹⁸ The righteous pray, and it is heard in the presence of the LORD; and from all their trouble he has delivered them. ¹⁹ The LORD is near to the brokenhearted; and the lowly in spirit he will redeem. ²⁰ Many evils encounter the righteous man; and from all of them the LORD delivers him. ²¹ He protects all his limbs; not one of them is broken. ²² The death of the wicked is bad, and those who hate the righteous man will be condemned. ²³ The LORD redeems the soul of his servants; and none who hope in his word are condemned. --

Spiritual Awareness

The spiritual rewrite for the verses is in bold.

Introduction and Superscript

This Psalm is based on events in David's life which are described in the Midrash Shocher Tov. David asked the LORD what the value of madness was? The LORD replied that someday in David's life, he will need to become mad. David had escaped Saul's wrath by fleeing to the land of the Philistines with nothing but the sword of Goliath. Goliath's brothers were the bodyguards of Achish, King of the Philistine city of Gath. The brothers recognized David and asked the King for permission to avenge Goliath by killing David. After some hesitation, the King agreed. David prayed to the LORD upon hearing this, asking him to give him madness, which he once criticized. David was given madness. He wrote that the King and Queen owed him money on the city gates. The daughters of the King went mad. They shouted and raved insanely inside the palace, and David ranted outside. The King drove David away to rid himself of David and his madness. Afterward, David composed this Psalm in gratitude for the madness. In the culture of David's day a person who was insane (mad) was not killed. It was believed that the person had an evil spirit in them. To kill the person could bring the evil spirit into the killer.

Verse 1

No matter what happened to David, He always praised the LORD.

I shall henceforth praise the LORD at all times; I will praise His mighty acts, which will continually remain in my mouth.

Verse 2

My soul glorifies in the LORD; let the humble hear it and be glad.

Verse 3

David called upon the unfortunate to rally with him as they together declared the greatness of the LORD.

The humble and I declare that greatness of the LORD, and together we exalt his Holy Name.

Verse 4

דָּרַשְׁתִּי (darash'tee) means "to seek with care." This word tells us that David sought instruction and inspiration from the LORD.

I sought the LORD, and He answered me, and delivered me from all my fears.

Verse 5

If you have the LORD in the center of your life you will discover that the LORD is a primary source of blessings and strength.

All people who looked unto the LORD received His power (His light), and their faces always shined the LORD's presence.

Verse 6 & 7

The poorest men who have sought out the LORD's help received it. That is a sign that the angel of the LORD encamps everywhere.

The poorest people cried out to the LORD, and He heard and has saved them from all troubles.

Thus, the angel of the LORD surrounds those who revere the LORD, and He has always delivered them.

Verse 8

This verse means that you should try to serve the LORD even if you have not decided to serve and follow the LORD. Then determine by your experience that the LORD is good.

Test the LORD for yourselves, and you shall see how good He is; how blessed are the people who trust in Him.

Verse 9

If a person feels that they belong to the LORD, they must demonstrate this desire and emotion. One must keep the LORD always in front of them (always living by His commandments).

O revere the LORD, you who are sanctified to Him, for there is no want to them that revere the LORD.

Verse 10

A person who does not place their lives into the hands of the LORD is like young lions who make physical desire their law and put their trust in their strength.

Young lions are poor and suffer hunger, but they who seek the LORD will never want for any good thing.

Verse 11

The psalmist offers words of advice. The following verses are addressed to young people. Materialism is not everything.

Come, O sons, hear me; I will teach you to revere the LORD.

Verse 12

Who is the person who desires life; who loves days that he may see good?

Verse 13

Keep your tongue from evil and your lips from deceitful language.

Verse 14

It is not always prudent to confront evil and fight against it. Sometimes it is better to avoid contact with it from the outset. Actively pursue good deeds fighting off the negative influences in the world. Sometimes the peaceful way is not the easy way.

Stay away from evil and always do good without hesitation; seek peace and pursue it.

Verses 15 & 16

These are promises from the LORD for those who follow Him and for evildoers.

The eyes of the LORD are looking at the righteous while His ear is open to their cry.

The countenance of the LORD is against people who commit evil and will cut off the memory of them from the earth.

Verses 17 & 18

The LORD does not limit his attention to only the righteous. He also responds to the cries of the humblest and downtrodden people.

Even the righteous cry, and the LORD hears them and delivers them out of all troubles.

The LORD is near the brokenhearted, and He saves such who are crushed in spirit.

Verses 19 & 20

The righteous people of the world who have been promised "life" and "good things" do not mean that they will never suffer. On the contrary, righteous people can expect significant troubles and calamities. These troubles are seen as a test of the righteous.

The righteous do suffer in life, but the LORD delivers them from it.

Verses 21 & 22

Disasters will eventually strike people who persist in their evil ways.

Evil will kill the lawless in the end, and they that hate the righteous shall be destroyed.

The LORD redeems the soul of His servants, and none of them who take refuge in Him shall be desolate.

Complete Psalm Rewrite Emphasizing Spiritual Awareness

By David, when he became mad (at his request from the LORD) so that he would be driven away by Abimelech the King of Gath.

I shall henceforth praise the LORD at all times; I will praise His mighty acts, which will continually remain in my mouth.

My soul glorifies in the LORD; let the humble hear it and be glad.
The humble and I declare that greatness of the LORD, and together we exalt his Holy Name.

I sought the LORD, and He answered me, and delivered me from all my fears.

All people who looked unto the LORD received His power (His light), and their faces always shined the LORD's presence.

The poorest people cried out to the LORD, and He heard and has saved them from all troubles.

Thus, the angel of the LORD surrounds those who revere the LORD, and He has always delivered them.

Test the LORD for yourselves, and you shall see how good He is; how blessed are the people who trust in Him.

O revere the LORD, you who are sanctified to Him, for there is no want to them that revere the LORD.

Young lions are poor and suffer hunger, but they who seek the LORD will never want for any good thing.

Come, O sons, hear me; I will teach you to revere the LORD.

Who is the person who desires life; who loves days that he may see good?

Keep your tongue from evil and your lips from deceitful language.

Stay away from evil and always do good without hesitation; seek peace and pursue it.

The eyes of the LORD are looking at the righteous while His ear is open to their cry.

The countenance of the LORD is against people who commit evil and will cut off the memory of them from the earth.

Even the righteous cry, and the LORD hears them and delivers them out of all troubles.

The LORD is near the brokenhearted, and He saves such who are crushed in spirit.

The righteous do suffer in life, but the LORD delivers them from it.

Evil will kill the lawless in the end, and they that hate the righteous shall be destroyed.

The LORD redeems the soul of His servants, and none of them who take refuge in Him shall be desolate.

61

Psalm 35

New American Standard 1995	Hebrew

Psa. 35:0 *A Psalm* of David.
 	
Psa. 35:1 Contend, O LORD, with those who [a]contend with me;
  Fight against those who [b]fight against me.
2 Take hold of [1][a]buckler and shield
  And rise up for [b]my help.
3 Draw also the spear and [1]the battle-axe to meet those who pursue me;
  Say to my soul, "I am [a]your salvation."
4 Let those be [a]ashamed and dishonored who seek my [1]life;
  Let those be [b]turned back and humiliated who devise evil against me.
5 Let them be [a]like chaff before the wind,
  With the angel of the LORD driving *them* on.
6 Let their way be dark and [a]slippery,
  With the angel of the LORD pursuing them.
7 For [a]without cause they [b]hid their net for me;
  Without cause they dug a [1]pit for my soul.
8 Let [a]destruction come upon him unawares,
  And [b]let the net which he hid catch himself;
  Into that very [c]destruction let him fall.
	לְדָוִד ׀ רִיבָה יְהוָה Psa. 35:1
	אֶת־יְרִיבַי לְחַם אֶת־לֹחֲמָי׃
	2 הַחֲזֵק מָגֵן וְצִנָּה וְקוּמָה
	בְּעֶזְרָתִי׃ 3 וְהָרֵק חֲנִית וּסְגֹר
	לִקְרַאת רֹדְפָי אֱמֹר לְנַפְשִׁי
	יְשֻׁעָתֵךְ אָנִי׃ 4 יֵבֹשׁוּ וְיִכָּלְמוּ
	מְבַקְשֵׁי נַפְשִׁי יִסֹּגוּ אָחוֹר
	וְיַחְפְּרוּ חֹשְׁבֵי רָעָתִי׃ 5 יִהְיוּ
	כְּמֹץ לִפְנֵי־רוּחַ וּמַלְאַךְ
	יְהוָה דּוֹחֶה׃ 6 יְהִי־דַרְכָּם
	חֹשֶׁךְ וַחֲלַקְלַקּוֹת וּמַלְאַךְ
	יְהוָה רֹדְפָם׃ 7 כִּי־חִנָּם
	טָמְנוּ־לִי שַׁחַת רִשְׁתָּם חִנָּם
	חָפְרוּ לְנַפְשִׁי׃ 8 תְּבוֹאֵהוּ
	שׁוֹאָה לֹא־יֵדָע וְרִשְׁתּוֹ
	אֲשֶׁר־טָמַן תִּלְכְּדוֹ בְּשׁוֹאָה
	יִפָּל־בָּהּ׃ 9 וְנַפְשִׁי תָּגִיל
	בַּיהוָה תָּשִׂישׂ בִּישׁוּעָתוֹ׃ 10
	כָּל עַצְמוֹתַי ׀ תֹּאמַרְנָה

Psa. 35:9   And my soul shall *a*rejoice in the LORD;

It shall *b*exult in His salvation.

10   All my *a*bones will say, "LORD, *b*who is like You,

Who delivers the afflicted from him *c*who is too strong for him,

And *d*the afflicted and the needy from him who robs him?"

11   *a*Malicious witnesses rise up;

They ask me of things that I do not know.

12   They *a*repay me evil for good,

To the bereavement of my soul.

13   But as for me, *a*when they were sick, my *b*clothing was sackcloth;

I *c*humbled my soul with fasting,

And my *d*prayer kept returning to my bosom.

14   I went about as though it were my friend or brother;

I *a*bowed down ¹mourning, as one who sorrows for a mother.

15   But *a*at my ¹stumbling they rejoiced and gathered themselves together;

The ²*b*smiters whom I did not know gathered together against me,

They ³*c*slandered me without ceasing.

16   Like godless jesters at a feast,

They *a*gnashed at me with their teeth.

Psa. 35:17   Lord, *a*how long will You look on?

Rescue my soul *b*from their ravages,

My *c*only *life* from the lions.

18   I will *a*give You thanks in the great congregation;

יְהוָה מִי כָמוֹךָ מַצִּיל עָנִי
מֵחָזָק מִמֶּנּוּ וְעָנִי וְאֶבְיוֹן
מִגֹּזְלוֹ ׃ 11 יְקוּמוּן עֵדֵי חָמָס
אֲשֶׁר לֹא־יָדַעְתִּי יִשְׁאָלוּנִי ׃
12 יְשַׁלְּמוּנִי רָעָה תַּחַת טוֹבָה
שְׁכוֹל לְנַפְשִׁי ׃ 13 וַאֲנִי |
בַּחֲלוֹתָם לְבוּשִׁי שָׂק עִנֵּיתִי
בַצּוֹם נַפְשִׁי וּתְפִלָּתִי עַל־
חֵיקִי תָשׁוּב ׃ 14 כְּרֵעַ־כְּאָח
לִי הִתְהַלָּכְתִּי כַּאֲבֶל־אֵם
קֹדֵר שַׁחוֹתִי ׃ 15 וּבְצַלְעִי
שָׂמְחוּ וְנֶאֱסָפוּ נֶאֶסְפוּ עָלַי
נֵכִים וְלֹא יָדַעְתִּי קָרְעוּ
וְלֹא־דָמּוּ ׃ 16 בְּחַנְפֵי לַעֲגֵי
מָעוֹג חָרֹק עָלַי שִׁנֵּימוֹ ׃ 17
אֲדֹנָי כַּמָּה תִּרְאֶה הָשִׁיבָה
נַפְשִׁי מִשֹּׁאֵיהֶם מִכְּפִירִים
יְחִידָתִי ׃ 18 אוֹדְךָ בְּקָהָל רָב
בְּעַם עָצוּם אֲהַלְלֶךָּ ׃ 19 אַל־
יִשְׂמְחוּ־לִי אֹיְבַי שֶׁקֶר שֹׂנְאַי
חִנָּם יִקְרְצוּ־עָיִן ׃ 20 כִּי לֹא

I will *b*praise You among a mighty throng.
19 *a*Do not let those who are wrongfully *b*my enemies rejoice over me;
Nor let those *c*who hate me without cause [1]*d*wink maliciously.
20 For they do not speak peace,
But they devise *a*deceitful words against those who are quiet in the land.
21 They *a*opened their mouth wide against me;
They said, "*b*Aha, aha, our eyes have seen it!"

Psa. 35:22 *a*You have seen it, O LORD, *b*do not keep silent;
O Lord, *c*do not be far from me.
23 *a*Stir up Yourself, and awake to my right
And to my cause, my God and my Lord.
24 *a*Judge me, O LORD my God, according to Your righteousness,
And *b*do not let them rejoice over me.
25 Do not let them say in their heart, "*a*Aha, our desire!"
Do not let them say, "We have *b*swallowed him up!"
26 Let *a*those be ashamed and humiliated altogether who rejoice at my distress;
Let those be *b*clothed with shame and dishonor who *c*magnify themselves over me.

Psa. 35:27 Let them *a*shout for joy and rejoice, who favor *b*my vindication;
And *c*let them say continually, "The LORD be magnified,

שָׁלוֹם יְדַבֵּרוּ וְעַל רִגְעֵי־
אֶרֶץ דִּבְרֵי מִרְמוֹת יַחֲשֹׁבוּן:
21 וַיַּרְחִיבוּ עָלַי פִּיהֶם אָמְרוּ
הֶאָח ׀ הֶאָח רָאֲתָה עֵינֵינוּ:
22 רָאִיתָה יְהוָה אַל־תֶּחֱרַשׁ
אֲדֹנָי אַל־תִּרְחַק מִמֶּנִּי: 23
הָעִירָה וְהָקִיצָה לְמִשְׁפָּטִי
אֱלֹהַי וַאדֹנָי לְרִיבִי: 24
שָׁפְטֵנִי כְצִדְקְךָ יְהוָה אֱלֹהָי
וְאַל־יִשְׂמְחוּ־לִי: 25 אַל־
יֹאמְרוּ בְלִבָּם הֶאָח נַפְשֵׁנוּ
אַל־יֹאמְרוּ בִּלַּעֲנוּהוּ: 26
יֵבֹשׁוּ וְיַחְפְּרוּ ׀ יַחְדָּו שְׂמֵחֵי
רָעָתִי יִלְבְּשׁוּ־בֹשֶׁת וּכְלִמָּה
הַמַּגְדִּילִים עָלָי: 27 יָרֹנּוּ
וְיִשְׂמְחוּ חֲפֵצֵי צִדְקִי וְיֹאמְרוּ
תָמִיד יִגְדַּל יְהוָה הֶחָפֵץ
שְׁלוֹם עַבְדּוֹ: 28 וּלְשׁוֹנִי
תֶּהְגֶּה צִדְקֶךָ כָּל־הַיּוֹם
תְּהִלָּתֶךָ:

Who [d]delights in the prosperity of His servant." 28 And [a]my tongue shall declare Your righteousness *And* Your praise all day long.	

References

Psalm 35:1
[a]Ps 18:43; Is 49:25
[b]Ps 56:2

Psalm 35:2
[1]I.e. small shield
[a]Ps 91:4
[b]Ps 44:26

Psalm 35:3
[1]Or *close up the path against those*
[a]Ps 62:2

Psalm 35:4
[1]Or *soul*
[a]Ps 70:2
[b]Ps 40:14; 129:5

Psalm 35:5
[a]Job 21:18; Ps 83:13; Is 29:5

Psalm 35:6
[a]Ps 73:18; Jer 23:12

Psalm 35:7
[1]*Pit* has been transposed from line above
[a]Ps 69:4; 109:3; 140:5
[b]Ps 9:15

Psalm 35:8
[a]Ps 55:23; Is 47:11; 1 Thess 5:3
[b]Ps 9:15
[c]Ps 73:18

Psalm 35:9
[a]Is 61:10
[b]Ps 9:14; 13:5; Luke 1:47

Psalm 35:10
[a]Ps 51:8
[b]Ex 15:11; Ps 86:8; Mic 7:18
[c]Ps 18:17
[d]Ps 37:14; 109:16

Psalm 35:11
[a]Ps 27:12

Psalm 35:12
[a]Ps 38:20; 109:5; Jer 18:20; John 10:32

Psalm 35:13
[a]Job 30:25
[b]Ps 69:11
[c]Ps 69:10
[d]Matt 10:13; Luke 10:6

Psalm 35:14
[1]Or *dressed in black*
[a]Ps 38:6

Psalm 35:15
[1]Or *limping*
[2]Or *smitten ones*
[3]Lit *tore*
[a]Obad 12
[b]Job 30:1, 8, 12
[c]Ps 7:2

Psalm 35:16
[a]Job 16:9; Ps 37:12; Lam 2:16

Psalm 35:17
[a]Ps 13:1; Hab 1:13
[b]Ps 35:7
[c]Ps 22:20, 21

Psalm 35:18
[a]Ps 22:22
[b]Ps 22:25

Psalm 35:19
[1]Or *wink the eye*
[a]Ps 13:4; 30:1; 38:16
[b]Ps 38:19; 69:4
[c]John 15:25
[d]Prov 6:13; 10:10

Psalm 35:20
[a]Ps 55:21; Jer 9:8; Mic 6:12

Psalm 35:21
[a]Job 16:10; Ps 22:13
[b]Ps 40:15; 70:3

Psalm 35:22
[a]Ex 3:7; Ps 10:14
[b]Ps 28:1
[c]Ps 10:1; 22:11; 38:21; 71:12

Psalm 35:23
[a]Ps 7:6; 44:23; 59:4; 80:2

Psalm 35:24
[a]Ps 9:4; 26:1; 43:1
[b]Ps 35:19

Psalm 35:25
[a]Ps 35:21
[b]Ps 56:1; 124:3; Prov 1:12; Lam 2:16

Psalm 35:26
[a]Ps 40:14
[b]Ps 109:29
[c]Job 19:5; Ps 38:16

Psalm 35:27
[a]Ps 32:11
[b]Ps 9:4
[c]Ps 40:16; 70:4
[d]Ps 147:11; 149:4

Psalm 35:28
[a]Ps 51:14; 71:15, 24

Targum

Psa. 35:1 Of David. Contend, O LORD, with those who contend against me; make war against those who war against me. [2] Take up a shield and buckler, and arise as my help. [3] And draw the spear and fasten the scabbard; and be prepared to meet those who pursue me; say to my soul, "I am your redeemer." [4] Let those who seek my life be ashamed and embarrassed; let those who plot my ruin shrink back and be subdued. [5] Let them be like chaff before the storm-wind, with the angel of the LORD repelling [them]. [6] May their paths be dark and murky, with the angel of the LORD pursuing them. [7] For without cause they have spread before me a pit; their net they have hidden for my soul without cause. [8] May a sudden calamity, unsuspected, overtake him; and may his net that he spread catch him; let him suddenly fall in it. [9] But my soul will rejoice in the word of the LORD; it will be glad in his redemption. [10] All my limbs will keep saying, "O LORD, who is like you?" – who saves the poor from the one stronger than he, and the poor and wretched from his oppressor. [11] Rapacious witnesses stand up; those whom I have not known question me. [12] They repay me evil for good, seeking to bereave my soul. [13] But I, in the time of their illness, wore sackcloth; I afflicted my soul with fasting; but my prayer will return to my bosom. [14] As if for my friend or brother, I went about like a mourner; like one who mourns for his mother, I was bowed down in gloom. [15] But when I was stricken, they rejoiced and even gathered together against me; the wicked, who belittle me with their words, and I knew it not, as if they cut my skin without drawing blood. [16] With smooth words and haughtiness and mockery, they grind their teeth against me. [17] O LORD, how long will you watch? Deliver my soul from their calamities, my body from the lion's whelps. [18] I will give thanks in your presence in the great assembly; among a mighty people I will praise you. [19] Let not my enemies rejoice over me [with] a lie – those who hate me without cause, winking with their eyes. [20] For they do not speak peace; and against the righteous of the earth who have rest in this world they plot devious things. [21] And they have opened their mouth wide against me [and] said, "Joy! Joy! Our eye has seen it!" [22] You have seen, O LORD, do not be silent; O LORD, be not far from me. [23] Wake and be alert to my cause, O my God; the LORD is the victor in my dispute. [24] Judge me by your generosity, O LORD my God, and they will not rejoice over me. [25] Let them not say in their heart, "Our soul is glad"; lest they say, "We have finished him." [26] Let those who rejoice at my harm be ashamed and subdued together; let those who vaunt themselves over me be clothed with shame and disgrace. [27] May those who seek my vindication be glad and rejoice and say always, "May the glory of the LORD be great, he who desires the peace of his servant." [28] And my tongue will sing of your generosity, all the day of your praise.

Spiritual Awareness

The spiritual rewrite for the verses are in bold.

Introduction

This psalm is about a hopeful declaration of David's beliefs in the LORD expressed in Psalm 34. David makes another request from the LORD to redeem him from the menace of his many enemies.

Verse 1

רִיבָה (reeva) – means "to strive, contend." The usage of this word indicates that there were enemies whose opposition to David and Israel was a part of their character and fundamental outlook on life. The struggle David was in was one-sided. He did not reciprocate against his enemies' hostilities. Today some people are antisemitic for no reason other than that it is a part of their character. Many of these people have little to no contact with Semitic people, yet they strive to hurt and destroy the Semitic race. This psalm applies to these modern-day persons.

By David. Strive, O LORD, with those that contend against me; fight against them that fight against me because of who I am.

Verse 2

הַחֲזֵק (hachazeaq) – means "be(come) strong, strengthen, prevail, harden, be courageous." In the context of this verse, this word refers to a shield that can repel missiles even if they are hurled from a great distance.

צִנָּה (sinnâ) – means "large shield." This word refers to a spiked shield used to ward off the direct, head-on attack.

Take hold of the shield and spiked shield and rise up to my help.

Verse 3

David is probably referring to a defensive weapon.

And draw out the spear and barrier against them who pursue me, saying to my soul that I am your salvation.

Verse 4, 5, and 6

David is asking the LORD to give him confidence that the LORD is indeed his salvation and that the hopes of David's enemies will never be fulfilled. David also asks the LORD to make his foes painfully aware of their own unworthiness and show them that killing David is against the LORD's plans.

Let them that seek after my soul be deceived in their hopes and become aware of their unworthiness; let them that devise my hurt fall back and find themselves unmasked.

Let them be as chaff before the wind as Your decree pushes them away.

Let their way be dark and slippery, so they stumble on the path as an angel of the LORD pursues them.

Verses 7 and 8

The standard maneuver for men of base malice was to project their own wickedness into the object of their hatred and then call it self-defense.

Let desolation come upon him unaware, and let his own snare which he secretly laid catch him; let him fall into it in desolation.

Then my soul will rejoice in the LORD; it will blissfully come into bloom in His salvation.

Verses 9 and 10

And my soul shall rejoice in the LORD; It shall exult in His salvation.

All my bones will say, "LORD, who is like You, who delivers the afflicted from him who is too strong for him, and the afflicted and the needy from him who robs him?

Verses 11 and 12

David describes the evil plans that his enemies have employed against him.

For they rise up as witnesses of violence, they call me to account for things of which I know nothing.

They repay me evil for good; they commit the crime of kidnapping upon my soul.

Verses 13 and 14

David mourned and fasted when his enemies were ill so that they might recover.

But as for me, even when they were sick, I mourned for them; I fasted, and as for my prayer at such times, may it return into my own bosom.

As if it had been my friend or my own brother, I went about; I bowed down sorrowfully as one mourns for his own mother.

Verse 15, 16, and 17

David said that even before he fell to the ground because he stumbled, his enemies were already rejoicing together.

But at my stumbling, they rejoiced and gathered themselves together; The smiters whom I did not know gathered together against me, they slandered me without ceasing.

Like godless jesters at a feast, they gnashed at me with their teeth.

Lord, how long will You look on? Rescue my soul from their ravages, my only *life* from the lions.

Verse 18 and 19

David said that whatever he experienced of the LORD's rule and presence on earth as shown by the fate of men, he would use it to spread the recognition and homage of the LORD with all peoples.

For I am to acknowledge You to the world; I am to proclaim You among the mighty people in praise of your mighty acts.

Let them not rejoice over me, those who are my enemies for an untrue cause; let them not look daggers who hate me without cause.

Verse 20

David claimed that his enemies stood up for the cause of the people's common welfare. They were not doing that; thus, they shamed themselves with this pretense.

For they try to fool the people with peace talks, and their deceitful speech concerning the critical moments of the land.

Verse 21

וַיַּרְחִיבוּ (yayar'cheevu) – means "and to be made wide" in the possessive form. This word occurs with an exclamation of malicious joy at another's misfortune. It is similar to an "aha!" moment.

While they opened their mouths wide against me, they say, Brother, O brother, ten our sees saw it at last.

Verse 22 and 23

You have seen it, O LORD, do not keep silent; O Lord, do not be far from me.

Stir up Yourself, and awake to my right and to my cause, my God and my Lord.

Verses 24, 25, 26, and 27

David does not appeal to the LORD for justice in general. He stays on the mission that the LORD had given to him. That mission was to become the King of Israel and prepare for the Temple's building at Jerusalem.

According to Your righteousness, judge me, O LORD my God, and do not let them rejoice over me.

Do not let them say in their heart, "Aha, our desire!" Do not let them say, "We have swallowed him up!"

Let those be ashamed and humiliated altogether who rejoice at my distress; Let those be clothed with shame and dishonor who magnify themselves over me.

Let them shout for joy and rejoice, who favor my vindication;
And let them say continually, "The LORD be magnified, who delights in the prosperity of His servant.

Verse 28

But my tongue shall meditate upon the proclamation of Your righteousness, and upon the praise of Your might acts all day long.

Complete Psalm Rewrite Emphasizing Spiritual Awareness

By David. Strive, O LORD, with those that contend against me; fight against them that fight against me because of who I am.

Take hold of the shield and spiked shield and rise up to my help.
And draw out the spear and barrier against them who pursue me, saying to my soul that I am your salvation.

Let them that seek after my soul be deceived in their hopes and become aware of their unworthiness; let them that devise my hurt fall back and find themselves unmasked.

Let them be as chaff before the wind as Your decree pushes them away.

Let their way be dark and slippery, so they stumble on the path as an angel of the LORD pursues them.

And my soul shall rejoice in the LORD; It shall exult in His salvation.

All my bones will say, "LORD, who is like You, who delivers the afflicted from him who is too strong for him, and the afflicted and the needy from him who robs him?

For they rise up as witnesses of violence, they call me to account for things of which I know nothing.

They repay me evil for good; they commit the crime of kidnapping upon my soul.

But as for me, even when they were sick, I mourned for them; I fasted, and as for my prayer at such times, may it return into my own bosom.

As if it had been my friend or my own brother, I went about; I bowed down sorrowfully as one mourns for his own mother.

But at my stumbling, they rejoiced and gathered themselves together; The smiters whom I did not know gathered together against me, they slandered me without ceasing.

Like godless jesters at a feast, they gnashed at me with their teeth.

Lord, how long will You look on? Rescue my soul from their ravages, my only *life* from the lions.

For I am to acknowledge You to the world; I am to proclaim You among the mighty people in praise of your mighty acts.

Let them not rejoice over me, those who are my enemies for an untrue cause; let them not look daggers who hate me without cause.

For they try to fool the people with peace talks, and their deceitful speech concerning the critical moments of the land.

While they opened their mouths wide against me, they say, Brother, O brother, ten our sees saw it at last.

You have seen it, O LORD, do not keep silent; O Lord, do not be far from me.

Stir up Yourself, and awake to my right and to my cause, my God and my Lord.

According to Your righteousness, judge me, O LORD my God, and do not let them rejoice over me.

Do not let them say in their heart, "Aha, our desire!" Do not let them say, "We have swallowed him up!"

Let those be ashamed and humiliated altogether who rejoice at my distress; Let those be clothed with shame and dishonor who magnify themselves over me.

Let them shout for joy and rejoice, who favor my vindication;

And let them say continually, "The LORD be magnified, who delights in the prosperity of His servant.

But my tongue shall meditate upon the proclamation of Your righteousness, and upon the praise of Your might acts all day long.

Psalm 36

New American Standard 1995	Hebrew
Psa. 36:0 For the choir director. *A Psalm* of David the servant of the LORD. **Psa. 36:1** Transgression speaks to the ungodly within [1]his heart; There is [a]no fear of God before his eyes. 2 For [1]it [a]flatters him in his *own* eyes Concerning the discovery of his iniquity *and* the hatred *of it.* 3 The [a]words of his mouth are wickedness and deceit; He has [b]ceased to [1]be wise *and* to do good. 4 He [a]plans wickedness upon his bed; He sets himself on a [b]path that is not good; He [c]does not despise evil. **Psa. 36:5** You're a lovingkindness, O LORD, [1]extends to the heavens, Your faithfulness *reaches* to the skies. 6 You're a righteousness is like the [1]mountains of God; Your [b]judgments are *like* a great deep. O LORD, You [c]preserve man and beast. 7 How [a]precious is Your loving-kindness, O God! And the children of men [b]take refuge in the shadow of Your wings. 8 They [a]drink their fill of the [1]abundance of Your house;	לַמְנַצֵּחַ ׀ לְעֶבֶד־ Psa. 36:1 יְהוָה לְדָוִד ׃ נְאֻם־פֶּשַׁע 2 לָרָשָׁע בְּקֶרֶב לִבִּי אֵין־פַּחַד אֱלֹהִים לְנֶגֶד עֵינָיו ׃ כִּי־ 3 הֶחֱלִיק אֵלָיו בְּעֵינָיו לִמְצֹא עֲוֺנוֹ לִשְׂנֹא ׃ דִּבְרֵי־פִיו אָוֶן 4 וּמִרְמָה חָדַל לְהַשְׂכִּיל לְהֵיטִיב ׃ אָוֶן ׀ יַחְשֹׁב עַל־ 5 מִשְׁכָּבוֹ יִתְיַצֵּב עַל־דֶּרֶךְ לֹא־טוֹב רָע לֹא יִמְאָס ׃ 6 יְהוָה בְּהַשָּׁמַיִם חַסְדֶּךָ אֱמוּנָתְךָ עַד־שְׁחָקִים ׃ 7 צִדְקָתְךָ ׀ כְּהַרְרֵי־אֵל מִשְׁפָּטֶךָ תְּהוֹם רַבָּה אָדָם־ 8 וּבְהֵמָה תוֹשִׁיעַ יְהוָה ׃ מַה־ 9 יָּקָר חַסְדְּךָ אֱלֹהִים וּבְנֵי אָדָם בְּצֵל כְּנָפֶיךָ יֶחֱסָיוּן ׃ 10 יִרְוְיֻן מִדֶּשֶׁן בֵּיתֶךָ וְנַחַל עֲדָנֶיךָ תַשְׁקֵם ׃ כִּי־עִמְּךָ 10 מְקוֹר חַיִּים בְּאוֹרְךָ נִרְאֶה־

And You give them to drink of the [b]river of Your delights.

9   For with You is the [a]fountain of life;

In Your light we see light.

Psa. 36:10   O continue Your loving-kindness to [a]those who know You,

And Your [b]righteousness to the upright in heart.

11   Let not the foot of pride come upon me,

And let not the hand of the wicked drive me away.

12   There the doers of iniquity have fallen;

They have been thrust down and [a]cannot rise.

אוֹר: 11 מְשֹׁךְ חַסְדְּךָ לְיֹדְעֶיךָ וְצִדְקָתְךָ לְיִשְׁרֵי־לֵב: 12 אַל־תְּבוֹאֵנִי רֶגֶל גַּאֲוָה וְיַד־רְשָׁעִים אַל־תְּנִדֵנִי: 13 שָׁם נָפְלוּ פֹּעֲלֵי אָוֶן דֹּחוּ וְלֹא־יָכְלוּ קוּם:

References

Psalm 36:1
[1]Another reading is *my heart*
[a]Rom 3:18

Psalm 36:2
[1]Or *he flatters himself*
[a]Deut 29:19; Ps 10:11; 49:18

Psalm 36:3
[1]Or *understand to do good*
[a]Ps 10:7; 12:2
[b]Ps 94:8; Jer 4:22

Psalm 36:4
[a]Prov 4:16; Mic 2:1
[b]Is 65:2
[c]Ps 52:3; Rom 12:9

Psalm 36:5
[1]Lit *is in*
[a]Ps 57:10; 103:11; 108:4

Psalm 36:6
[1]Or *mighty mountains*
[a]Ps 71:19
[b]Job 11:8; Ps 77:19; Rom 11:33
[c]Neh 9:6; Ps 104:14, 15; 145:16

Psalm 36:7
[a]Ps 40:5; 139:17
[b]Ruth 2:12; Ps 17:8; 57:1; 91:4

Psalm 36:8
[1]Lit *fatness*
[a]Ps 63:5; 65:4; Is 25:6; Jer 31:12-14
[b]Job 20:17; Ps 46:4; Rev 22:1

Psalm 36:9
[a]Jer 2:13

Psalm 36:10
[a]Jer 22:16
[b]Ps 24:5

Psalm 36:12
[a]Ps 140:10; Is 26:14

Targum

Psa. 36:1 For praise. Of the servant of the LORD, David. [2] Rebellion said to the sinner within my heart, "There is no fear of the LORD before his eyes." [3] Because he flatters him with his eyes to find sins, to hate instruction. [4] The words of his mouth are wickedness and deceit; he has ceased to be wise in doing good. [5] Wickedness plots on his bed; he will take his stand in a way not good; he will not reject evil. [6] O LORD, your goodness is in the heaven of heavens, your faithfulness reaches to the skies. [7] Your righteousness is as high as the great mountains; your judgments are as deep as the great abyss; you will redeem both the sons of men and beasts, O LORD. [8] How precious is your goodness, O LORD; and the sons of men will dwell securely in the shadow of your presence. [9] They will drink deeply of the plenteous blessings of your house; and you will let them drink of your pleasant fountain. [10] For with you are streams of living water; in the splendor of your glory we will see light. [11] Extend your goodness over those who know you; and your generosity over the upright of heart. [12] May the foot of the proud not reach me; and may the hands of the wicked not make me wander. [13] There fell those who commit falsehood; they will be struck down, and will not rise again. --

Spiritual Awareness

The spiritual rewrite for the verses is in bold.

Introduction

This Psalm shows a stark contrast between people who follow the ways of the LORD and those who defy the LORD. The sage Radak said that the villain in this Psalm is Evil Inclination. Evil inclination is that spirit that drives people to do evil. David offers the philosophy that motivated the actions and attitudes of evil people in his day.

Superscript

For the choir director. A Psalm of David, the servant of the LORD.

Verse 1

נְאֻם (n'um) means "to speak." This word is a divine word. Therefore, the speaker is always the LORD. Several words in Hebrew are only used when the sentence is referring to the LORD.

An evil person tells him/herself that if the omnipotent LORD did not desire evil in this creation, He certainly would prevent it from happening. The LORD could also prevent evil from happening by making it unattractive. Thus, there is no fear that the LORD will do something to evil people. Therefore they commit their sins.

It is the LORD's pronouncement that transgression speaks to what is lawless in the heart; there is no of Gevurah before an evil person's eyes.

Verse 2

The wicked person believes that the LORD has paved the way for him/her to reach their sinful goals and pursue with bitter hatred anyone who might stand in his/her way.

For in his eyes, the LORD has smoothed the path so that he/she can attain their sinful goal and maybe hated.

Verse 3

More importantly, a sinful person uses their words to continue sin and conceal their true views and intentions.

The words of his mouth are violence and deceit; he has ceased to apply his mind to doing good.

Verse 4

Evil people spend their lives in the service of Evil Inclination. Even when they are sleeping, they plot how best to use their physical and mental faculties for evil purposes. An evil person plans to be on an evil path.

Even on his bed, he resolutely puts himself on the path to evil, and he does not scorn evil.

Verse 5

Chesed shines the LORD's loving-kindness from the Earth to the Heavens. The LORD offers his rules that train people in moral perfection and thus receive future salvation. Evil people do not understand that Evil inclination was given glamor only to lure people. The LORD gave humanity the ability to practice evil by its own free will. Every person can refuse the temptations of Evil inclination.

O LORD, Chesed's loving-kindness reaches the Earth and extends back into Heaven.

Verse 6

The LORD knows that every generation of humanity still needs training on how to be righteous. Chesed is constantly sending its power to train humans.

The Sefirah Chesed is like the mighty mountains, and Your judgments are like the great deep; man and beast You will preserve, O LORD.

Verse 7

This verse is a parallelism of verse six. Chesed shines its power of loving-kindness upon the children of men.

The Sefirah Chesed shows the LORD's loving-kindness. The children of men find refuge in the shadow of Your wings.

Verse 8 & 9

The righteous received an abundance of delights from the LORD through the Divine Law and the sanctification of life, which they learn and attain. Wicked people may think that they are satisfied with the materialism of life. They will never understand that it is spiritual life that is better.

They satisfy themselves from the abundance of Your House, and You make them drink from the rivers of Your pleasures.

For with You is the fountain of life; in Your spiritual power, we see that power.

Verse 10

מְשֹׁךְ חַסְדְּךָ (m'shoch chas'd'cha) – means "continue loving-kindness." This phrase is generally used to express the prolonged deferment of fulfilling a promise or a stipulation.

Defer your loving-kindness to them that know You, and grant your righteousness to those that are upright in heart.

Verse 11

Defer your loving-kindness to them that know You, and grant your righteousness to those that are upright in heart.

Verse 12

Evil people may think that their abundance of fortune and power is true happiness. However, it is their path to hopeless destruction.

It is there that the works of violence have fallen; they have been thrust down and cannot rise.

Complete Psalm Rewrite Emphasizing Spiritual Awareness

For the choir director. A Psalm of David, the servant of the LORD.

It is the LORD's pronouncement that transgression speaks to what is lawless in the heart; there is no of Gevurah before an evil person's eyes.

For in his eyes, the LORD has smoothed the path so that he/she can attain their sinful goal and maybe hated.

The words of his mouth are violence and deceit; he has ceased to apply his mind to doing good.

Even on his bed, he resolutely puts himself on the path to evil, and he does not scorn evil.

O LORD, Chesed's loving-kindness reaches the Earth and extends back into Heaven.

The Sefirah Chesed is like the mighty mountains, and Your judgments are like the great deep; man and beast You will preserve, O LORD.

The Sefirah Chesed shows the LORD's loving-kindness. The children of men find refuge in the shadow of Your wings.

They satisfy themselves from the abundance of Your House, and You make them drink from the rivers of Your pleasures.

For with You is the fountain of life; in Your spiritual power, we see that power.

Defer your loving-kindness to them that know You, and grant your righteousness to those that are upright in heart.

It is there that the works of violence have fallen; they have been thrust down and cannot rise.

Psalm 37

New American Standard 1995	Hebrew

Psa. 37:0 *A Psalm* of David.

Psa. 37:1 *a*Do not fret because of evildoers,
Be not *b*envious toward wrongdoers.
2   For they will *a*wither quickly like the grass
And *b*fade like the green herb.
3   *a*Trust in the LORD and do good;
*b*Dwell in the land and *1c*cultivate faithfulness.
4   *a*Delight yourself in the LORD;
And He will *b*give you the desires of your heart.
5   *a*Commit your way to the LORD,
Trust also in Him, and He will do it.
6   He will bring forth *a*your righteousness as the light
And your judgment *b*as the noonday.

Psa. 37:7 *1*Rest in the LORD and *a*wait *2*patiently for Him;
*b*Do not fret because of him who *c*prospers in his way,
Because of the man who carries out wicked schemes.
8   Cease from anger and *a*forsake wrath;
Do not fret; *it leads* only to evildoing.
9   For *a*evildoers will be cut off,
But those who wait for the LORD, they will *b*inherit the land.

לְדָוִד ׀ אַל־תִּתְחַר Psa. 37:1

בַּמְּרֵעִים אַל־תְּקַנֵּא בְּעֹשֵׂי

עַוְלָה: 2 כִּי כֶחָצִיר מְהֵרָה

יִמָּלוּ וּכְיֶרֶק דֶּשֶׁא יִבּוֹלוּן: 3

בְּטַח בַּיהוָה וַעֲשֵׂה־טוֹב

שְׁכָן־אֶרֶץ וּרְעֵה אֱמוּנָה: 4

וְהִתְעַנַּג עַל־יְהוָה וְיִתֶּן־לְךָ

מִשְׁאֲלֹת לִבֶּךָ: 5 גּוֹל עַל־

יְהוָה דַּרְכֶּךָ וּבְטַח עָלָיו

וְהוּא יַעֲשֶׂה: 6 וְהוֹצִיא

כָאוֹר צִדְקֶךָ וּמִשְׁפָּטֶךָ

כַּצָּהֳרָיִם: 7 דּוֹם ׀ לַיהוָה

וְהִתְחוֹלֵל לוֹ אַל־תִּתְחַר

בְּמַצְלִיחַ דַּרְכּוֹ בְּאִישׁ עֹשֶׂה

מְזִמּוֹת: 8 הֶרֶף מֵאַף וַעֲזֹב

חֵמָה אַל־תִּתְחַר אַךְ־

לְהָרֵעַ: 9 כִּי־מְרֵעִים יִכָּרֵתוּן

וְקֹוֵי יְהוָה הֵמָּה יִירְשׁוּ־

אָרֶץ: 10 וְעוֹד מְעַט וְאֵין

10 Yet [a]a little while and the wicked man will be no more;

And you will look carefully for [b]his place and he will not be *there*.

11 But [a]the humble will inherit the land

And will delight themselves in [b]abundant prosperity.

Psa. 37:12 The wicked [a]plots against the righteous

And [b]gnashes at him with his teeth.

13 The Lord [a]laughs at him,

For He sees [b]his day is coming.

14 The wicked have drawn the sword and [a]bent their bow

To cast down the [b]afflicted and the needy,

To [c]slay those who are upright in conduct.

15 Their sword will enter their own heart,

And their [a]bows will be broken.

Psa. 37:16 [a]Better is the little of the righteous

Than the abundance of many wicked.

17 For the [a]arms of the wicked will be broken,

But the LORD [b]sustains the righteous.

18 The LORD [a]knows the days of the [1]blameless,

And their [b]inheritance will be forever.

19 They will not be ashamed in the time of evil,

And [a]in the days of famine they will have abundance.

רָשָׁע וְהִתְבּוֹנַנְתָּ עַל־מְקוֹמוֹ וְאֵינֶנּוּ׃ 11 וַעֲנָוִים יִירְשׁוּ־אָרֶץ וְהִתְעַנְּגוּ עַל־רֹב שָׁלוֹם׃ 12 זֹמֵם רָשָׁע לַצַּדִּיק וְחֹרֵק עָלָיו שִׁנָּיו׃ 13 אֲדֹנָי יִשְׂחַק־לוֹ כִּי־רָאָה כִּי־יָבֹא יוֹמוֹ׃ 14 חֶרֶב ׀ פָּתְחוּ רְשָׁעִים וְדָרְכוּ קַשְׁתָּם לְהַפִּיל עָנִי וְאֶבְיוֹן לִטְבוֹחַ יִשְׁרֵי־דָרֶךְ׃ 15 חַרְבָּם תָּבוֹא בְלִבָּם וְקַשְּׁתוֹתָם תִּשָּׁבַרְנָה׃ 16 טוֹב־מְעַט לַצַּדִּיק מֵהֲמוֹן רְשָׁעִים רַבִּים׃ 17 כִּי זְרוֹעוֹת רְשָׁעִים תִּשָּׁבַרְנָה וְסוֹמֵךְ צַדִּיקִים יְהוָה׃ 18 יוֹדֵעַ יְהוָה יְמֵי תְמִימִם וְנַחֲלָתָם לְעוֹלָם תִּהְיֶה׃ 19 לֹא־יֵבֹשׁוּ בְּעֵת רָעָה וּבִימֵי רְעָבוֹן יִשְׂבָּעוּ׃ 20 כִּי רְשָׁעִים ׀ יֹאבֵדוּ וְאֹיְבֵי יְהוָה כִּיקַר כָּרִים כָּלוּ בֶעָשָׁן כָּלוּ׃ 21 לֹוֶה רָשָׁע וְלֹא

²⁰ But the ^awicked will perish;
And the enemies of the LORD
will be like the ¹glory of the pastures,
They vanish — ^blike smoke they
vanish away.
²¹ The wicked borrows and does not
pay back,
But the righteous ^ais gracious and
gives.
²² For ^athose blessed by Him will
^binherit the land,
But those ^ccursed by Him will be
cut off.

Psa. 37:23 ^aThe steps of a man
are established by the LORD,
And He ^bdelights in his way.
²⁴ When ^ahe falls, he will not be
hurled headlong,
Because ^bthe LORD is the One
¹who holds his hand.
²⁵ I have been young and now I am
old,
Yet ^aI have not seen the righteous
forsaken
Or ^bhis ¹descendants begging
bread.
²⁶ All day long ^ahe is gracious and
lends,
And ^bhis ¹descendants are a
blessing.

Psa. 37:27 ^aDepart from evil
and do good,
¹So you will abide ^bforever.
²⁸ For the LORD ^aloves ¹justice
And ^bdoes not forsake His godly
ones;
They are ^cpreserved forever,
But the ^{2d}descendants of the
wicked will be cut off.

22 יְשַׁלֵּם וְצַדִּיק חוֹנֵן וְנוֹתֵן׃
כִּי מְבֹרָכָיו יִירְשׁוּ אָרֶץ
וּמְקֻלָּלָיו יִכָּרֵתוּ׃ 23 מֵיְהוָה
מִצְעֲדֵי־גֶבֶר כּוֹנָנוּ וְדַרְכּוֹ
יֶחְפָּץ׃ 24 כִּי־יִפֹּל לֹא־יוּטָל
כִּי־יְהוָה סוֹמֵךְ יָדוֹ׃ 25 נַעַר
הָיִיתִי גַּם־זָקַנְתִּי וְלֹא־
רָאִיתִי צַדִּיק נֶעֱזָב וְזַרְעוֹ
מְבַקֶּשׁ־לָחֶם׃ 26 כָּל־הַיּוֹם
חוֹנֵן וּמַלְוֶה וְזַרְעוֹ לִבְרָכָה׃
27 סוּר מֵרָע וַעֲשֵׂה־טוֹב
וּשְׁכֹן לְעוֹלָם׃ 28 כִּי יְהוָה ׀
אֹהֵב מִשְׁפָּט וְלֹא־יַעֲזֹב אֶת־
חֲסִידָיו לְעוֹלָם נִשְׁמָרוּ וְזֶרַע
רְשָׁעִים נִכְרָת׃ 29 צַדִּיקִים
יִירְשׁוּ־אָרֶץ וְיִשְׁכְּנוּ לָעַד
עָלֶיהָ׃ 30 פִּי־צַדִּיק יֶהְגֶּה
חָכְמָה וּלְשׁוֹנוֹ תְּדַבֵּר
מִשְׁפָּט׃ 31 תּוֹרַת אֱלֹהָיו
בְּלִבּוֹ לֹא תִמְעַד אֲשֻׁרָיו׃ 32
צוֹפֶה רָשָׁע לַצַּדִּיק וּמְבַקֵּשׁ

29 The righteous will *a*inherit the land

And *b*dwell in it forever.

30 The mouth of the righteous *a*utters wisdom,

And his tongue *b*speaks justice.

31 The *a*law of his God is in his heart;

His *b*steps do not slip.

32 The *a*wicked spies upon the righteous

And *b*seeks to kill him.

33 The LORD will *a*not leave him in his hand

Or *b*let him be condemned when he is judged.

34 *a*Wait for the LORD and keep His way,

And He will exalt you to inherit the land;

When the *b*wicked are cut off, you will see it.

Psa. 37:35 I have *a*seen a wicked, violent man

Spreading himself like a *b*luxuriant [1]tree in its native soil.

36 Then [1]he passed away, and lo, he *a*was no more;

I sought for him, but he could not be found.

37 Mark the [1]*a*blameless man, and behold the *b*upright;

For the man of peace will have a [2]*c*posterity.

38 But transgressors will be altogether *a*destroyed;

The [1]posterity of the wicked will be *b*cut off.

39 But the *a*salvation of the righteous is from the LORD;

לַהֲמִיתֽוֹ׃ ³³ יְהוָה לֹא־
יַעַזְבֶ֣נּוּ בְיָד֑וֹ וְלֹ֥א יַ֝רְשִׁיעֶ֗נּוּ
בְּהִשָּׁפְטֽוֹ׃ ³⁴ קַוֵּ֤ה אֶל־יְהוָ֨ה
וּשְׁמֹ֬ר דַּרְכּ֗וֹ וִֽירֽוֹמִמְךָ֮
לָרֶ֪שֶׁת אָ֥רֶץ בְּהִכָּרֵ֖ת רְשָׁעִ֣ים
תִּרְאֶֽה׃ ³⁵ רָ֭אִיתִי רָשָׁ֣ע
עָרִ֑יץ וּ֝מִתְעָרֶ֗ה כְּאֶזְרָ֥ח
רַעֲנָֽן׃ ³⁶ וַֽ֭יַּעֲבֹר וְהִנֵּ֣ה אֵינֶ֑נּוּ
וָֽ֝אֲבַקְשֵׁ֗הוּ וְלֹ֣א נִמְצָֽא׃ ³⁷
שְׁמָר־תָּ֭ם וּרְאֵ֣ה יָשָׁ֑ר כִּֽי־
אַחֲרִ֖ית לְאִ֣ישׁ שָׁלֽוֹם׃ ³⁸
וּֽפֹשְׁעִים֮ נִשְׁמְד֪וּ יַ֫חְדָּ֥ו
אַחֲרִ֖ית רְשָׁעִ֣ים נִכְרָֽתָה׃ ³⁹
וּתְשׁוּעַ֣ת צַ֭דִּיקִים מֵיְהוָ֑ה
מָ֝עוּזָּ֗ם בְּעֵ֣ת צָרָֽה׃ ⁴⁰
וַֽיַּעְזְרֵ֥ם יְהוָ֗ה וַֽיְפַ֫לְּטֵ֥ם
יְפַלְּטֵ֣ם מֵ֭רְשָׁעִים וְֽיוֹשִׁיעֵ֑ם
כִּי־חָ֥סוּ בֽוֹ׃

He is their strength [b]in time of trouble.
40   [a]The LORD helps them and delivers them;
He [b]delivers them from the wicked and saves them,
Because they [c]take refuge in Him.

References

Psalm 37:1
[a]Prov 23:17; 24:19
[b]Ps 73:3; Prov 3:31

Psalm 37:2
[a]Job 14:2; Ps 90:6; 92:7; James 1:11
[b]Ps 129:6

Psalm 37:3
[1]Or *feed securely* or *feed on His faithfulness*
[a]Ps 62:8
[b]Deut 30:20
[c]Is 40:11; Ezek 34:13, 14

Psalm 37:4
[a]Job 22:26; Ps 94:19; Is 58:14
[b]Ps 21:2; 145:19; Matt 7:7, 8

Psalm 37:5
[a]Ps 55:22; Prov 16:3; 1 Pet 5:7

Psalm 37:6
[a]Ps 97:11; Is 58:8, 10; Mic 7:9
[b]Job 11:17

Psalm 37:7
[1]Or *Be still*
[2]Or *longingly*
[a]Ps 40:1; 62:5; Lam 3:26
[b]Ps 37:1, 8
[c]Jer 12:1

Psalm 37:8
[a]Eph 4:31; Col 3:8

Psalm 37:9
[a]Ps 37:2, 22
[b]Ps 25:13; Prov 2:21; Is 57:13; 60:21; Matt 5:5

Psalm 37:10
[a]Job 24:24
[b]Job 7:10; Ps 37:35, 36

Psalm 37:11
[a]Matt 5:5
[b]Ps 72:7

Psalm 37:12
[a]Ps 31:13, 20
[b]Ps 35:16

Psalm 37:13
[a]Ps 2:4
[b]1 Sam 26:10; Job 18:20

Psalm 37:14
[a]Ps 11:2; Lam 2:4
[b]Ps 35:10; 86:1
[c]Ps 11:2

Psalm 37:15
[a]1 Sam 2:4; Ps 46:9

Psalm 37:16
[a]Prov 15:16; 16:8

Psalm 37:17
[a]Job 38:15; Ps 10:15; Ezek 30:21
[b]Ps 71:6; 145:14

Psalm 37:18
[1]Lit *complete; or perfect*
[a]Ps 1:6; 31:7
[b]Ps 37:27, 29

Psalm 37:19
[a]Job 5:20; Ps 33:19

Psalm 37:20
[1]I.e. flowers
[a]Ps 73:27
[b]Ps 68:2; 102:3

Psalm 37:21
[a]Ps 112:5, 9

Psalm 37:22
[a]Prov 3:33
[b]Ps 37:9
[c]Job 5:3

Psalm 37:23
[a]1 Sam 2:9; Ps 40:2; 66:9; 119:5
[b]Ps 147:11

Psalm 37:24
[1]Or *who sustains him with His hand*
[a]Ps 145:14; Prov 24:16; Mic 7:8
[b]Ps 147:6

Psalm 37:25
[1]Lit *seed*
[a]Ps 37:28; Is 41:17; Heb 13:5
[b]Ps 109:10

Psalm 37:26
[1]Lit *seed*
[a]Deut 15:8; Ps 37:21
[b]Ps 147:13

Psalm 37:27
[1]Or *And dwell forever*
[a]Ps 34:14
[b]Ps 37:18; 102:28

Psalm 37:28
[1]Lit *judgment*
[2]Lit *seed*
[a]Ps 11:7; 33:5
[b]Ps 37:25
[c]Ps 31:23
[d]Ps 21:10; 37:9; Prov 2:22; Is 14:20

Psalm 37:29
[a]Ps 37:9; Prov 2:21
[b]Ps 37:18

Psalm 37:30
[a]Ps 49:3; Prov 10:13
[b]Ps 101:1; 119:13

Psalm 37:31
[a]Deut 6:6; Ps 40:8; 119:11; Is 51:7; Jer 31:33
[b]Ps 26:1; 37:23

Psalm 37:32
[a]Ps 10:8; 17:11
[b]Ps 37:14

Psalm 37:33
[a]Ps 31:8; 2 Pet 2:9
[b]Ps 34:22; 109:31

Psalm 37:34
[a]Ps 27:14; 37:9
[b]Ps 52:5, 6; 91:8

Psalm 37:35
[1]Lit *native;* Heb obscure
[a]Job 5:3; Jer 12:2
[b]Job 8:16

Psalm 37:36
[1]Ancient versions read *I passed by*
[a]Job 20:5; Ps 37:10

Psalm 37:37
[1]Lit *complete;* or *perfect*
[2]Lit *an end*
[a]Ps 37:18
[b]Ps 7:10
[c]Is 57:1, 2

Psalm 37:38
[1]Lit *end*
[a]Ps 1:4-6; 37:20, 28
[b]Ps 37:9; 73:17

Psalm 37:39
[a]Ps 3:8; 62:1
[b]Ps 9:9; 37:19

Psalm 37:40
[a]Ps 54:4
[b]Ps 22:4; Is 31:5; Dan 3:17; 6:23
[c]1 Chr 5:20; Ps 34:22

Targum

Psa. 37:1 Of David. Have no desire for malefactors, to be like them; and do not be jealous of those who commit oppression, to join with them. **2** Because their end will be like plants, quickly will they wither; and like the green grass they will fall away. **3** Trust in the word of the LORD and do good; dwell in the land and be strong in faith. **4** And you will delight in the LORD, and he will give you the requests of your heart. **5** Reveal to the LORD your ways, and trust in his word, and he will act. **6** And your righteousness will come out like light, and your judgment like noonday. **7** Be quiet in the presence of the LORD and wait for him; do not desire the wicked man who prospers his way, the man who follows the counsel of sinners. **8** Wait without anger and forsake wrath; do not long indeed to do evil. **9** For those who do evil will be destroyed; but those who hope in the word of the LORD – they will inherit the land. **10** And yet a little while, and there is no wicked man; you will look carefully at his place, and he is not. **11** But the humble will inherit the land; and they will delight in the plenitude of peace. **12** The wicked man plots harm against the righteous man, and grinds his teeth against him. **13** The LORD will laugh at him, for he has seen, for the day of his ruin has come. **14** The wicked have drawn the sword and bent their bows to kill the humble and lowly, to slaughter the upright of way. **15** Their blade will enter their [own] heart, and their bows will break. **16** Better in the presence of the LORD is the smallness of the righteous man than the multitude of many wicked men. **17** For the arms of the wicked will be broken, but the word of the LORD supports the righteous. **18** The days of the blameless are known in the LORD's presence, and their inheritance will last forever. **19** They will not be ashamed in the time of evil, and in the days of famine they are satisfied. **20** For the wicked will perish, and the enemies of the LORD are like the glory of young sheep that at first are fattened but finally slaughtered – likewise the wicked will perish and be destroyed in the smoke of Gehenna. **21** The wicked borrows and does not repay; but the righteous is compassionate, and gives. 22 For those who are blessed by his word will inherit the land; but those who are cursed by death will be destroyed. 23 In the presence of the LORD the steps of a man are made firm, and he will favor his ways. 24 For when he falls into sickness, he will not die, because the LORD is the helper at his hand. 25 I was a boy, but have grown old; and I have not seen the righteous man abandoned or his sons seeking bread because of want. 26 For all the day he is compassionate and lends; and his seed is for a blessing. 27 Turn from evil, and practice kindness, and abide for eternal life. [ANOTHER TARGUM: Turn from doing evil, O righteous man, and do good; because of this you will abide forever.] 28 For the LORD loves justice and will not abandon his pious ones; they are protected forever; but the sons of the wicked will be destroyed. 29 The righteous will inherit the land, and will dwell on it forever. 30 The mouth of the righteous murmurs wisdom, and his tongue speaks justice. 31 The law (nimus) of his God is in his heart; his feet do not stumble. 32 The wicked man observes the righteous man and seeks to kill him. 33 The LORD will not abandon him into his hand, and will not find him guilty when he is judged. [ANOTHER TARGUM: When he stands in judgment.] 34 Hope in the word of the LORD, and keep his way, and he will raise you up to inherit the land; you will see the destruction of the wicked. 35 I have seen the wicked man, strong and mighty, like a native and leafy tree. 36 And he ceased from the world, and, behold, he is no more; and I sought him but he was not found. 37 Preserve blamelessness, and behold, honesty; for the end of [such] a son of man is peace. 38 But rebels will be destroyed together; the end of the wicked is destruction. 39 But the redemption of the righteous is from the presence of the LORD, their strength in the time of trouble. 40 And the LORD helped them and saved them, he saved them from sinners; and he will redeem them, for they trusted in his word.

Spiritual Awareness

Introduction

In this Psalm, David described the forces of evil which strive to convince humans that there is no God. Evil people point to their success as evidence that no Supreme Being is watching what they are doing.

Verse one

Do not become perturbed because wicked people seem to have good fortune. Gevurah will issue punishment on the wicked in time. It is challenging to watch evil people break the laws of the LORD and the government, and they get away with it. Where is divine intervention? The Zohar says that the LORD gives evil people time to correct their evil ways and ask for repentance. Unfortunately, there are plenty of people who never change their ways. Guvurah may not affect them in their lifetime, but the LORD tells us that Guvurah will get involved on judgment day. Sins that are not unrepented will appear on the list that the LORD will use on judgment day. The righteous will have an empty list. The wicked will have a long list. Keep faith in the LORD that justice will happen.

Verse two

Green herbs ripen shortly after they are planted. This plant does not grow deep, sturdy roots in the soil. They ripen and die quickly.

Verse three

Have faith in the LORD because you will feel secure and aware of His presence. The LORD loves the people who want to belong to Him and follow His Torah.

Verse four

Seek and find your greatest joy in the presence of the LORD. The heart's desire is the need to feel that the LORD is surrounding righteous people.

Verse five

This verse is a parallel verse to verse four. Parallel verses are repeated verses for emphasis. Why would you place yourself on any path that the LORD has not laid out for you?

Verse six

This verse reminds us that one must commit their life to the LORD. Trust in the LORD that He is watching out for you.

Verse seven

One should refrain from all speech, complaints, and protests about wicked people. The fate of the righteous will at times seem incomprehensible. One must accept that wicked people will get away with their evil, and the righteous cannot do anything to stop it.

Verse eight

This is a parallel verse to verse seven.

Verse nine

Evildoers' apparent success with help brings about their eventual downfall. Wait for the LORD to send Gevurah upon the evildoers. The new Heaven and earth will be for the righteous. The wicked will be cased out to Sheol.

Verse ten

The life of the wicked is usually short. If their evil comes to light within the confines of the government's law, then they will be punished by their peers. It is true that there were and are wicked people who live long lives and stay out of the bounds of the government's laws. Gevurah will eventually punish these people.

Verse eleven

In time the righteous and wicked will be separated, and the wicked will be cast into Sheol.

Verse twelve to fifteen

The ways of the righteous people infuriate wicked people—the wicked stand in opposition to the righteous. Eventually, Gevurah will step in and assist the wicked to destroy themselves.

Verse sixteen

מֵהֲמוֹן (mehamon) – means "abundance" or "sound." David could have referred to the abundance of property the wicked accumulate or the noise that they make. Wicked people tend to complain about everything that does not entirely fit into their expectations. The LORD likes the sound of the righteous person's voice and dislikes the noise of the wicked.

Verse seventeen

This verse repeats earlier verses. Gevurah will break the arms of the wicked as they are judged and sent to Sheol.

Verse eighteen

The LORD is aware of the wicked and will give them their inheritance. That inheritance is an eternity in the depths of Sheol.

Verse nineteen

Wicked people do not feel ashamed for their evil during their lives. Usually, wicked people justify their actions as righteous. They will never accept that their ways were evil. Thus, they never repent, for they are not ashamed. Unfortunately, during famine days, they will not go hungry because they have accumulated what they need to survive. That is fine for that time. The righteous know that wicked peoples' final journey is to Sheol, and they will be cut off from the LORD's love and grace forever.

Verse twenty

This verse describes the penalty for the wicked as described in verse nineteen.

Verse twenty-one

Everything a person owns is a gift from the LORD. Eventually, life ends, and the properties and monies one accumulates over a lifetime will go to someone else. Righteous people understand this. They also understand that blessings that shower down from Heaven are meant to be shared with other people.

Verse twenty-two

The divine blessing of eternal life with the LORD in Heaven will be won through a life of following the ways of the Torah.

Verse twenty-three & twenty-four

The righteous person walks in the steps that the LORD has laid out. The wicked person walks in the steps that he/she decides to follow.

Verse twenty-five

In the years of David's life from birth to when he wrote this Psalm, he never witnessed a righteous person forsaken by the LORD.

Verse twenty-six

When the LORD sends blessings from Heaven, the righteous person will share those blessings with his/her fellow human.

Verse twenty-seven through twenty-nine

Always do good and avoid evil. By doing so, the righteous will dwell with the LORD forever.

Verse thirty

Wisdom comes to the righteous.

Verse thirty-one

The righteous person is wise being full of wisdom because the Torah is in his/her heart.

Verse thirty-two

Evil people are the implacable foe of the righteous because of the difference in their philosophies of life and their attitudes toward their neighbors. Loving one's neighbor means that one never cheats or steals from their neighbor. The wicked see no problem stealing and cheating from their neighbor.

Verse thirty-three

If a wicked person captures a righteous person, the LORD will not leave the righteous person in the hands of the adversary. The LORD will not let the righteous be condemned when the world reaches the final judgment from Gevurah.

Verse thirty-four

There will be a day when the wicked are removed from the earth and sent to Sheol. The LORD will give the righteous the new Heaven and new earth when that day comes.

Verse thirty-five

David said that he had witnessed wicked people, yet they seemed to prosper.

Verse thirty-six

When a wicked person dies, that person is disconnected from the LORD because the person is sent to Sheol.

Verse thirty-seven through forty

These verses summarize the Psalm. Wicked people may look prosperous, but there will come a time when Gevurah will judge them and send them to Sheol. In Sheol, they will be disconnected from the LORD for eternity. The righteous may not possess as many material things, but they will be filled with spiritual things. They will eventually live an eternity with the LORD.

Psalm 38

New American Standard 1995	Hebrew
Psa. 38:0 A Psalm of David, for a memorial.	מִזְמוֹר לְדָוִד לְהַזְכִּיר׃ יְהוָה [2]
Psa. 38:1 O LORD, [a]rebuke me not in Your wrath, And chasten me not in Your burning anger.	אַל־בְּקֶצְפְּךָ תוֹכִיחֵנִי וּבַחֲמָתְךָ תְיַסְּרֵנִי׃ כִּי־חִצֶּיךָ נִחֲתוּ בִי [3]
[2] For Your [a]arrows have sunk deep into me, And [b]Your hand has pressed down on me.	וַתִּנְחַת עָלַי יָדֶךָ׃ אֵין־מְתֹם [4]
[3] There is [a]no soundness in my flesh [b]because of Your indignation; There is no health [c]in my bones because of my sin.	בִּבְשָׂרִי מִפְּנֵי זַעְמֶךָ אֵין־שָׁלוֹם בַּעֲצָמַי מִפְּנֵי חַטָּאתִי׃ כִּי [5]
[4] For my [a]iniquities are gone over my head; As a heavy burden they weigh too much for me.	עֲוֺנֹתַי עָבְרוּ רֹאשִׁי כְּמַשָּׂא כָבֵד יִכְבְּדוּ מִמֶּנִּי׃ הִבְאִישׁוּ נָמַקּוּ [6]
[5] My [1]wounds grow foul *and* fester Because of [a]my folly.	חַבּוּרֹתָי מִפְּנֵי אִוַּלְתִּי׃ נַעֲוֵיתִי [7]
[6] I am bent over and [a]greatly bowed down; I [b]go mourning all day long.	שַׁחֹתִי עַד־מְאֹד כָּל־הַיּוֹם קֹדֵר הִלָּכְתִּי׃ כִּי־כְסָלַי מָלְאוּ [8]
[7] For my loins are filled with [a]burning, And there is [b]no soundness in my flesh.	נִקְלֶה וְאֵין מְתֹם בִּבְשָׂרִי׃ [9]
[8] I am [a]benumbed and [1]badly crushed; I [2b]groan because of the [3]agitation of my heart.	נְפוּגוֹתִי וְנִדְכֵּיתִי עַד־מְאֹד שָׁאַגְתִּי מִנַּהֲמַת לִבִּי׃ אֲדֹנָי [10]
Psa. 38:9 Lord, all [a]my desire is [1]before You;	נֶגְדְּךָ כָל־תַּאֲוָתִי וְאַנְחָתִי מִמְּךָ לֹא־נִסְתָּרָה׃ לִבִּי סְחַרְחַר [11] עֲזָבַנִי כֹחִי וְאוֹר־עֵינַי גַּם־הֵם אֵין אִתִּי׃ אֹהֲבַי וְרֵעַי מִנֶּגֶד [12] נִגְעִי יַעֲמֹדוּ וּקְרוֹבַי מֵרָחֹק עָמָדוּ׃ וַיְנַקְשׁוּ מְבַקְשֵׁי [13] נַפְשִׁי וְדֹרְשֵׁי רָעָתִי דִּבְּרוּ הַוּוֹת

And my ᵇsighing is not hidden from You.

10 My heart throbs, ᵃmy strength fails me;

And the ᵇlight of my eyes, even ¹that ²has gone from me.

11 My ¹ᵃloved ones and my friends stand aloof from my plague;

And my kinsmen ᵇstand afar off.

12 Those who ᵃseek my life ᵇlay snares *for me;*

And those who ᶜseek to injure me have ¹threatened destruction,

And they ᵈdevise treachery all day long.

Psa. 38:13 But I, like a deaf man, do not hear;

And *I am* like a ᵃmute man who does not open his mouth.

14 Yes, I am like a man who does not hear,

And in whose mouth are no arguments.

15 For ᵃI ¹hope in You, O LORD;

You ᵇwill answer, O Lord my God.

16 For I said, "May they not rejoice over me,

Who, when my foot slips, ᵃwould magnify themselves against me."

17 For I am ᵃready to fall,

And ᵇmy ¹sorrow is continually before me.

18 For I ¹ᵃconfess my iniquity;

I am full of ᵇanxiety because of my sin.

19 But my ᵃenemies are vigorous *and* ¹strong,

And many are those who ᵇhate me wrongfully.

וּמִרְמ֔וֹת כָּל־הַיּ֥וֹם יֶהְגּֽוּ׃ 14

וַאֲנִ֣י כְחֵרֵשׁ֮ לֹ֤א אֶשְׁמָ֥ע וּכְאִלֵּ֑ם 15 וָאֱהִ֗י כְּאִ֗ישׁ

אֲשֶׁ֥ר לֹא־שֹׁמֵ֑עַ וְאֵ֥ין בְּפִ֗יו

תּוֹכָחֽוֹת׃ 16 כִּֽי־לְךָ֣ יְהוָ֣ה

הוֹחָ֑לְתִּי אַתָּ֥ה תַעֲנֶ֗ה אֲדֹנָ֥י

אֱלֹהָֽי׃ 17 כִּֽי־אָ֭מַרְתִּי פֶּן־

יִשְׂמְחוּ־לִ֑י בְּמ֥וֹט רַ֝גְלִ֗י עָלַ֥י

הִגְדִּֽילוּ׃ 18 כִּֽי־אֲ֭נִי לְצֶ֣לַע נָכ֑וֹן

וּמַכְאוֹבִ֖י נֶגְדִּ֣י תָמִֽיד׃ 19 כִּֽי־

20 עֲוֺנִ֥י אַגִּ֑יד אֶ֝דְאַ֗ג מֵֽחַטָּאתִֽי׃

וְאֹיְבַ֣י חַ֭יִּים עָצֵ֑מוּ וְרַבּ֖וּ שֹׂנְאַ֣י

שָֽׁקֶר׃ 21 וּמְשַׁלְּמֵ֣י רָ֭עָה תַּ֣חַת

טוֹבָ֑ה יִ֝שְׂטְנ֗וּנִי תַּ֣חַת רְדוֹפִי־

[רָדְפִי־]ט֥וֹב׃ 22 אַל־תַּֽעַזְבֵ֥נִי

יְהוָ֑ה אֱ֝לֹהַ֗י אַל־תִּרְחַ֥ק מִמֶּֽנִּי׃

23 ח֥וּשָׁה לְעֶזְרָתִ֑י אֲ֝דֹנָ֗י

תְּשׁוּעָתִֽי׃

<table>
<tr><td>

20   And those who [a]repay evil for good,

     They [b]oppose me, because I follow what is good.

21   Do not forsake me, O LORD;

     O my God, [a]do not be far from me!

22   Make [a]haste to help me,

     O Lord, [b]my salvation!

</td><td></td></tr>
</table>

References

Psalm 38:1 *a*Ps 6:1	**Psalm 38:10** ¹Lit *they have* ²Lit *is not with me* *a*Ps 31:10 *b*Ps 6:7; 69:3; 88:9
Psalm 38:2 *a*Job 6:4 *b*Ps 32:4	**Psalm 38:11** ¹Or *lovers* *a*Ps 31:11; 88:18 *b*Luke 23:49
Psalm 38:3 *a*Is 1:6 *b*Ps 102:10 *c*Job 33:19; Ps 6:2; 31:10	**Psalm 38:12** ¹Lit *spoken* *a*Ps 54:3 *b*Ps 140:5 *c*Ps 35:4 *d*Ps 35:20
Psalm 38:4 *a*Ezra 9:6; Ps 40:12	**Psalm 38:13** *a*Ps 39:2, 9
Psalm 38:5 ¹Or *stripes* *a*Ps 69:5	**Psalm 38:15** ¹Or *wait for* *a*Ps 39:7 *b*Ps 17:6
Psalm 38:6 *a*Ps 35:14 *b*Job 30:28; Ps 42:9; 43:2	**Psalm 38:16** *a*Ps 35:26
Psalm 38:7 *a*Ps 102:3 *b*Ps 38:3	**Psalm 38:17** ¹Lit *pain* *a*Ps 35:15 *b*Ps 13:2
Psalm 38:8 ¹Or *greatly* ²Lit *roar* ³Lit *growling* *a*Lam 1:13, 20f; 2:11; 5:17 *b*Job 3:24; Ps 22:1; 32:3	
Psalm 38:9 ¹Or known *to You* *a*Ps 10:17 *b*Ps 6:6; 102:5	**Psalm 38:18** ¹Or *declare* *a*Ps 32:5 *b*2 Cor 7:9, 10

Psalm 38:19
[1]Or *numerous*
[a]Ps 18:17
[b]Ps 35:19

Psalm 38:20
[a]Ps 35:12
[b]Ps 109:5; 1 John 3:12

Psalm 38:21
[a]Ps 22:19; 35:22

Psalm 38:22
[a]Ps 40:13, 17
[b]Ps 27:1

Targum

Psa. 38:1 A psalm of David. A handful of incense, a good memorial for Israel. ² O LORD, do not rebuke me in your anger, and do not punish me in your wrath. ³ For your arrows have descended on me, and the blow of your hand rests upon me. ⁴ There is no healing in my body because of your anger, no health in my limbs because of my sin. ⁵ For my sins have mounted past my head; like a heavy burden, they were too heavy for me. ⁶ My wounds stank, they decayed, because of my foolishness. ⁷ I am bent over, I am greatly bowed down; all the day I have gone about in gloom. ⁸ For my loins are filled with burning, and there is no healing in my body. ⁹ I have become faint and I have been humbled greatly; I moaned because of the groaning of my heart. ¹⁰ O LORD, before you is all my desire; and my sighing is not hid from you. ¹¹ My heart has become hot; my strength has left me, and the light of my eyes – even they are not with me. ¹² My friends and companions stood away from the sight of my plague; and my relatives stand far off. ¹³ And those who seek my life have made traps; and those who seek my ruin have uttered lies, and they murmur deceit all the day. ¹⁴ But I am like a deaf man, I will not hear, like a mute who does not open his mouth. ¹⁵ And I have become like a man who has never heard, and there is no rebuke in his mouth. ¹⁶ For in your presence, O LORD, have I prayed; you will accept [my prayer], O LORD my God. ¹⁷ For I said, "Lest they rejoice over me." When my foot stumbled, they vaunted themselves over me. ¹⁸ For I am prepared for disaster, and my pain is before me always. ¹⁹ For my sin I will relate, I will be troubled by my sin. ²⁰ But my enemies, alive, have grown strong; those who hate me through deceit are numerous. ²¹ And those who repay evil for good oppose me, because I have pursued good. ²² Do not forsake me, O LORD; my God, do not be far from me. ²³ Hasten to my aid, O LORD, my redemption.

Spiritual Awareness

The spiritual rewrite for the verses is in bold.

Introduction

Psalms 38 to 41 are the concluding Psalms of the Psalms' first book. These psalms deal with one theme – the illness that David was afflicted with due to his sins. David tried to learn something from the illnesses and shared these lessons through these psalms.

Superscript

הַזְכִּיר (haz'keer) – means "to remind." The NASB translates this word as "memorial." The Theological Word Book of the Old Testament says, "think (about), meditate (upon), pay attention (to); remember, recollect; mention, declare, recite, proclaim, invoke, commemorate, accuse, confess." David wrote this psalm to pass along what he learned during his illness.

A Psalm of David, for all to know.

Verse One & Two

David acknowledges that his sin is the cause of the illness that he has to live through.

O LORD, do not reprimand me with Your wrath and do not discipline me with your fierce anger.

For Your arrows go deep into me even when Your hand only comes down up me.

Verse three

David understood that it was not an illness that made him feel sick but rather the guilt of his sin.

My flesh has no soundness because of Your indignation; there is no health in my bones because of my sin.

Verse four

David said that a present sin made him recall all of his past sins.

For my iniquities are gone over my head; like an onerous burden, they are too heavy for me.

Verse five

These wounds could have been boils that festered and rotted because his body could not heal them. This illness was caused because his sins had deprived David of his spiritual and moral strength.

My boils fester until they rot because of my sin.

Verse Six

David acknowledged that his physical weakness was because of his moral folly.

Therefore, I cringed and was greatly bowed down; I went around all day with my spirit overcast.

Verse seven

For my loins are filled with burning, and there is no soundness in my flesh.

Verse eight

נְפוּגוֹתִי (n'phugotee) – means "I grow weak," or "I cease."

I grow weak and was sorely oppressed; I groaned from the moaning of my heart.

Verse nine

Even though David was a sinner, he still called the LORD his Master. David believed that his sin caused his illness. Instead of becoming angry with the LORD, he acknowledged that the sin was the cause and it was his fault. David took responsibility for his actions.

My Master, all my yearning is before You, and my sighing is not hidden from you.

Verse Ten

My heart wanders hither and yon, my strength has failed me, even the light of my eyes is gone from me.

Verse Eleven and Twelve

David's friends and relatives had abandoned him. This action allowed his enemies to gain new courage to slander and defame him.

My friends and my companions stand aloof from my sufferings, and my kinsmen stand afar off.

Those who seek my life lay snares for me; And those who seek to injure me have threatened destruction, And they devise treachery all day long.

Verses thirteen to sixteen

David said that he kept silent in the face of the slander and defamation from his enemies. He feared that if he would attempt to refute them, he might become provoked and be carried away to do something that the LORD might not approve.

But I, like a deaf man, do not hear; And I am like a mute man who does not open his mouth.

Yes, I am like a man who does not hear, and in whose mouth are no arguments.

For I hope in You, O LORD; You will answer, O Lord my God.

For I said, "May they not rejoice over me, who, when my foot slips, would magnify themselves against me."

Verse seventeen & eighteen

For, as for me, I was prepared for disaster, and my pain is continually before me.

Because I realized my inequity, and was full of worry because of my sin.

Verses nineteen & twenty

David's enemies were deeply steeped in sin, and its removal did not trouble them. They did not care what sins they committed as long as the sins were directed toward David.

But my enemies are vigorous *and* strong, and many are those who hate me wrongfully.

And those who repay evil for good, they oppose me, because I follow what is good.

Verse twenty-one and twenty-two

David felt confident that he would win the final victory over his enemies because he kept his faith in the LORD.

Do not forsake me, O LORD, you are my God and be close to me.

Hasten to help me; You are my Master and my salvation

Complete Psalm Rewrite Emphasizing Spiritual Awareness

A Psalm of David, for all to know.

O LORD, do not reprimand me with Your wrath and do not discipline me with your fierce anger.

For Your arrows go deep into me even when Your hand only comes down up me.

My flesh has no soundness because of Your indignation; there is no health in my bones because of my sin.

For my iniquities are gone over my head; like an onerous burden, they are too heavy for me.

My boils fester until they rot because of my sin.

Therefore, I cringed and was greatly bowed down; I went around all day with my spirit overcast.

For my loins are filled with burning, and there is no soundness in my flesh.
My Master, all my yearning is before You, and my sighing is not hidden from you.

My heart wanders hither and yon, my strength has failed me, even the light of my eyes is gone from me.

My friends and my companions stand aloof from my sufferings, and my kinsmen stand afar off.

Those who seek my life lay snares for me; And those who seek to injure me have threatened destruction, And they devise treachery all day long.

But I, like a deaf man, do not hear; And I am like a mute man who does not open his mouth.

Yes, I am like a man who does not hear, and in whose mouth are no arguments.

For I hope in You, O LORD; You will answer, O Lord my God.

For I said, "May they not rejoice over me, who, when my foot slips, would magnify themselves against me."

For, as for me, I was prepared for disaster, and my pain is continually before me.

Because I realized my inequity, and was full of worry because of my sin.

But my enemies are vigorous *and* strong, and many are those who hate me wrongfully.

And those who repay evil for good, they oppose me, because I follow what is good.

Do not forsake me, O LORD, you are my God and be close to me.

Hasten to help me; You are my Master and my salvation

Psalm 39

New American Standard 1995	Hebrew
Psa. 39:0 For the choir director, for †Jeduthun. A Psalm of David. **Psa. 39:1** I said, "I will *a*guard my ways That I *b*may not sin with my tongue; I will guard *c*my mouth as with a muzzle While the wicked are in my presence." 2 I was *a*mute [1]and silent, I [2]refrained *even* from good, And my [3]sorrow grew worse. 3 My *a*heart was hot within me, While I was musing the fire burned; *Then* I spoke with my tongue: 4 "LORD, make me to know *a*my end And what is the extent of my days; Let me know how *b*transient I am. 5 "Behold, You have made *a*my days *as* handbreadths, And my *b*lifetime as nothing in Your sight; Surely every man [1]at his best is [2]a mere *c*breath. [3]Selah. 6 "Surely every man *a*walks about as [1]a phantom; Surely they make an *b*uproar for nothing; He *c*amasses *riches* and does not know who will gather them.	לַמְנַצֵּחַ לִידִיתוּן Psa. 39:1 [לִ][ידוּתוּן] מִזְמוֹר לְדָוִד׃ 2 אָמַרְתִּי אֶשְׁמְרָה דְרָכַי מֵחֲטוֹא בִלְשׁוֹנִי אֶשְׁמְרָה לְפִי מַחְסוֹם בְּעֹד רָשָׁע לְנֶגְדִּי׃ נֶאֱלַמְתִּי 3 דוּמִיָּה הֶחֱשֵׁיתִי מִטּוֹב וּכְאֵבִי נֶעְכָּר׃ חַם־לִבִּי ׀ בְּקִרְבִּי 4 בַּהֲגִיגִי תִבְעַר־אֵשׁ דִּבַּרְתִּי בִּלְשׁוֹנִי׃ הוֹדִיעֵנִי יְהֹוָה ׀ קִצִּי 5 וּמִדַּת יָמַי מַה־הִיא אֵדְעָה מֶה־ חָדֵל אָנִי׃ הִנֵּה טְפָחוֹת ׀ 6 נָתַתָּה יָמַי וְחֶלְדִּי כְאַיִן נֶגְדֶּךָ אַךְ כָּל־הֶבֶל כָּל־אָדָם נִצָּב סֶלָה׃ אַךְ־בְּצֶלֶם ׀ יִתְהַלֶּךְ־ 7 אִישׁ אַךְ־הֶבֶל יֶהֱמָיוּן יִצְבֹּר וְלֹא־יֵדַע מִי־אֹסְפָם׃ וְעַתָּה 8 מַה־קִּוִּיתִי אֲדֹנָי תּוֹחַלְתִּי לְךָ הִיא׃ מִכָּל־פְּשָׁעַי הַצִּילֵנִי 9 חֶרְפַּת נָבָל אַל־תְּשִׂימֵנִי׃ 10 נֶאֱלַמְתִּי לֹא אֶפְתַּח־פִּי כִּי אַתָּה עָשִׂיתָ׃ הָסֵר מֵעָלַי 11 נִגְעֶךָ מִתִּגְרַת יָדְךָ אֲנִי כָלִיתִי׃

Psa. 39:7 "And now, Lord, for what do I wait?

My [a]hope is in You.

8 "[a]Deliver me from all my transgressions;

Make me not the [b]reproach of the foolish.

9 "I have become [a]mute, I do not open my mouth,

Because it is [b]You who have done *it*.

10 "[a]Remove Your plague from me;

Because of [b]the opposition of Your hand I am [1]perishing.

11 "With [a]reproofs You chasten a man for iniquity;

You [b]consume as a moth what is precious to him;

Surely [c]every man is a mere breath. Selah.

Psa. 39:12 "[a]Hear my prayer, O LORD, and give ear to my cry;

Do not be silent [b]at my tears;

For I am [c]a stranger with You,

A [d]sojourner like all my fathers.

13 "[a]Turn Your gaze away from me, that I may [1]smile *again*

Before I depart and am no more."

בְּתוֹכָחוֹת עַל־עָוֺן ׀ וַיִּסֶּר תָּ 12
אִישׁ וַתֶּמֶס כָּעָשׁ חֲמוּדוֹ אַךְ
הֶבֶל כָּל־אָדָם סֶלָה ׃ שִׁמְעָה־ 13
תְפִלָּתִי ׀ יְהֹוָה וְשַׁוְעָתִי ׀
הַאֲזִינָה אֶל־דִּמְעָתִי אַל־תֶּחֱרַשׁ
כִּי גֵר אָנֹכִי עִמָּךְ תּוֹשָׁב כְּכָל־
אֲבוֹתָי ׃ הָשַׁע מִמֶּנִּי וְאַבְלִיגָה 14
בְּטֶרֶם אֵלֵךְ וְאֵינֶנִּי ׃

References

Psalm 39:1
[a]1 Kin 2:4; 2 Kin 10:31; Ps 119:9
[b]Job 2:10; Ps 34:13; James 3:5-12
[c]Ps 141:3; James 3:2

Psalm 39:2
[1]Lit *with silence*
[2]Lit *kept silence*
[3]Lit *pain*
[a]Ps 38:13

Psalm 39:3
[a]Ps 32:4; Jer 20:9; Luke 24:32

Psalm 39:4
[a]Job 6:11; Ps 90:12; 119:84
[b]Ps 78:39; 103:14

Psalm 39:5
[1]Lit *standing firm*
[2]Or *altogether vanity*
[3]*Selah* may mean: *Pause, Crescendo* or *Musical interlude*
[a]Ps 89:47
[b]Ps 144:4
[c]Job 14:2; Ps 62:9; Eccl 6:12

Psalm 39:6
[1]Lit *an image*
[a]1 Cor 7:31; James 1:10, 11; 1 Pet 1:24
[b]Ps 127:2; Eccl 5:17
[c]Ps 49:10; Eccl 2:26; 5:14; Luke 12:20

Psalm 39:7
[a]Ps 38:15

Psalm 39:8
[a]Ps 51:9, 14; 79:9
[b]Ps 44:13; 79:4; 119:22

Psalm 39:9
[a]Ps 39:2
[b]2 Sam 16:10; Job 2:10

Psalm 39:10
[1]Or *wasting away*
[a]Job 9:34; 13:21
[b]Ps 32:4

Psalm 39:11
[a]Ezek 5:15; 2 Pet 2:16
[b]Job 13:28; Ps 90:7; Is 50:9
[c]Ps 39:5

Psalm 39:12
[a]Ps 102:1; 143:1
[b]2 Kin 20:5; Ps 56:8
[c]Lev 25:23; 1 Chr 29:15; Ps 119:19; Heb 11:13; 1 Pet 2:11
[d]Gen 47:9

Psalm 39:13
[1]Or *become cheerful*
[a]Job 7:19; 10:20, 21; 14:6; Ps 102:24

Targum

Psa. 39:1 For praise; concerning the guard of the sanctuary, according to Jeduthun. A Psalm of David. [2] I said, I will keep my way from sinning by my tongue, I will keep a bridle for my mouth, while there is a wicked man before me. [3] I was dumb, I was quiet, I kept away from the words of Torah; because of this my pain contorts [me]. [4] My heart grew heated in my body; when I murmur, fire will burn; I spoke with my tongue. [5] Make known to me the way of my end; and the measure of my days, what they are; I would know when I will cease from the world. [6] Behold, you have ordained my days to be swift, and my body is as nothing before you. Truly, all are considered to be nothing, but all the righteous endure for eternal life. [7] Truly, in the image of the LORD man goes about; truly for nothing they are perplexed; he gathers and does not know why anyone gathers them. [8] And now, why have I hoped, O LORD? My waiting is for you. [9] From all my rebellions deliver me; do not put on me the shame of the fool. [10] I have become mute, and I will not open my mouth, for you have done it. [11] Remove your plague from me; I am destroyed by the blow of your mighty hand. [12] You punish a son of man with rebuke for sin; and you have dissolved his body like wool that has been nibbled away; truly every son of man is as nothing forever. [13] Receive my prayer, O LORD, and hear my supplication, and to my tears do not be silent; for I am like a foreigner with you, an alien like all my fathers. [14] Leave me alone, and I will depart, ere I go and exist no more.

Spiritual Awareness

The spiritual rewrite for the verses is in bold.

Superscript

This Psalm conveys the dismal mood of a crushed man shrouded in the gloom of his failures and defeat. According to Rabbi Hirsch יְדִיתוּן is not the name of a person. He compared the Hebrew word structure and noted that it is the same as Psalm 77. It is not easy to understand his relationship with David if this is a name. This name can be found in 1 Chronicles 16:41-42. It is not clear from this passage if Jeduthun was the choir director. Therefore, Hirsch believes that Jeduthun is not a name.

יְדִיתוּן (ydeeton) root word means "hand" and in its form denotes the activity of the hand. It means the eternally constant Divine providence as demonstrated in the fate of individuals.

To Him Who grants strength to master the providences of the LORD's hand, a Psalm of David.

Verse one

David said he resolved to guard his conduct not to do anything that the LORD may object. Every word that David said was to glorify the LORD.

I thought I will care to my ways that I will not sin with my tongue (my words); I will be careful with what comes out of the mouth while the wicked are in my presence.

Verse two

David's silence was due to his having attained peace of mind. He suppressed every thought of good, this good fortune. This silence did not soothe David. His pain became all the greater for having kept silent.

Then I became silent as if I had been soothed; I kept silent regarding the good, but my pain was all the more grievous for it.

Verse three

David's silence agitated him to the point that he could not remain silent.

My heart grew hot within me; the fire kindled on my brooding – then I spoke with my tongue.

Verse four

David saw the unjust distribution of possessions in the world. This process made him contemplate the true purpose of human life. Was it just good fortune that some people have more than others? He wondered if material possessions had any bearing on a person's ultimate destination.

LORD make me recognize my goals and what the measure of my days is, for I wish to know the extent of my days.

Verse five

טְפָחוֹת (t'fachot) – can be translated as "handbreadths" as is done in the NASB. It means a "fit's breadth." This word can also mean "span." David acknowledged that human life was brief, especially when compared to the age of the Universe.

Behold, You may make my days a span, and my short-lived existence is as nothing before you; Certainly, every man at his best is a mere breath. Meditate on this verse.

Verse six

The purpose of human existence is to resemble the LORD as closely as possible. Every word and action a person takes should contribute to being spiritually and morally equivalent to what the LORD would say and do.

Surely every person should conduct themselves in likeness to the LORD; and it is only for vanity that they are in turmoil; he heaps up riches and does not know who will gather them in.

Verse seven

David said that since he gained an understanding of the world's ways, he no longer yearns for material possessions.

And now, what is it I wait for? My hope is in You.

Verse eight

This verse is a twofold plea. The first is David asking to receive all the chastisement that he believed would remove the temptation to sin against the LORD. The second is to let him retain his spiritual and moral fortitude even in the face of suffering. The suffering was intended to teach him right from wrong.

Deliver me from all my transgressions, and make me not the laughingstock among the degenerate.

Verse nine

I have become mute, I do not open my mouth because it is You who have done it.

Verse ten

David asked the LORD to spare him the fate intended to train and discipline him. He knew that he had to endure these sufferings; however, he prayed that the LORD remove these things,

Remove Your plague from me; I have wasted away from the blow of Your hand.

Verse eleven

It was not the desire of the LORD to let humans perish because of the punishments. Instead, the judgment of Gevurah was to train humans to better behavior.

You have chastised every human for iniquity with rebukes by letting that which was close to his heart be consumed as if by moths; therefore, there is futility in every human. Meditate on this verse.

Verse 12 & 13

David realized that his time on the Earth was short. He was to be prepared and trained to live in Heaven for eternity during his time here.

Therefore hear my prayer, O LORD, incline your ear to my cry; keep not silent at my tear, for I am a stranger here with You. A sojourner as all my fathers were.

Turn away from me so that I may recover before I go away and am here no more.

Complete Psalm Rewrite Emphasizing Spiritual Awareness

To Him Who grants strength to master the providences of the LORD's hand, a Psalm of David.

I thought I will care to my ways that I will not sin with my tongue (my words); I will be careful with what comes out of the mouth while the wicked are in my presence.

Then I became silent as if I had been soothed; I kept silent regarding the good, but my pain was all the more grievous for it.

My heart grew hot within me; the fire kindled on my brooding – then I spoke with my tongue.

LORD make me recognize my goals and what the measure of my days is, for I wish to know the extent of my days.

Behold, You may make my days a span, and my short-lived existence is as nothing before you; Certainly, every man at his best is a mere breath. Meditate on this verse.

Surely every person should conduct themselves in likeness to the LORD; and it is only for vanity that they are in turmoil; he heaps up riches and does not know who will gather them in.

And now, what is it I wait for? My hope is in You.

Deliver me from all my transgressions, and make me not the laughingstock among the degenerate.

I have become mute, I do not open my mouth because it is You who have done it.

Remove Your plague from me; I have wasted away from the blow of Your hand.

You have chastised every human for iniquity with rebukes by letting that which was close to his heart be consumed as if by moths; therefore, there is futility in every human. Meditate on this verse.

Therefore hear my prayer, O LORD, incline your ear to my cry; keep not silent at my tear, for I am a stranger here with You. A sojourner as all my fathers were.

Turn away from me so that I may recover before I go away and am here no more.

Psalm 40

New American Standard 1995	Hebrew
Psa. 40:0 For the choir director. A Psalm of David.	לַמְנַצֵּחַ לְדָוִד Psa. 40:1
Psa. 40:1 I [a]waited [1]patiently for the LORD; And He inclined to me and [b]heard my cry. 2 He brought me up out of the [a]pit of destruction, out of the [1]miry clay, And [b]He set my feet upon a rock [c]making my footsteps firm. 3 He put a [a]new song in my mouth, a song of praise to our God; Many will [b]see and fear And will trust in the LORD.	מִזְמוֹר ׃ 2 קַוֹּה קִוִּיתִי יְהוָה וַיֵּט אֵלַי וַיִּשְׁמַע שַׁוְעָתִי ׃ 3 וַיַּעֲלֵנִי ׀ מִבּוֹר שָׁאוֹן מִטִּיט הַיָּוֵן וַיָּקֶם עַל־סֶלַע רַגְלַי כּוֹנֵן אֲשֻׁרָי ׃ 4 וַיִּתֵּן בְּפִי ׀ שִׁיר חָדָשׁ תְּהִלָּה לֵאלֹהֵינוּ יִרְאוּ רַבִּים וְיִירָאוּ וְיִבְטְחוּ בַּיהוָה ׃ 5 אַשְׁרֵי הַגֶּבֶר
Psa. 40:4 How [a]blessed is the man who has made the LORD his trust, And [b]has not [1]turned to the proud, nor to those who [c]lapse into falsehood. 5 Many, O LORD my God, are [a]the wonders which You have done, And Your [b]thoughts toward us; There is none to compare with You. If I would declare and speak of them, They [c]would be too numerous to count.	אֲשֶׁר־שָׂם יְהוָה מִבְטַחוֹ וְלֹא־פָנָה אֶל־רְהָבִים וְשָׂטֵי כָזָב ׃ 6 רַבּוֹת עָשִׂיתָ ׀ אַתָּה ׀ יְהוָה אֱלֹהַי נִפְלְאֹתֶיךָ וּמַחְשְׁבֹתֶיךָ אֵלֵינוּ אֵין ׀ עֲרֹךְ אֵלֶיךָ אַגִּידָה וַאֲדַבֵּרָה עָצְמוּ מִסַּפֵּר ׃ 7 זֶבַח וּמִנְחָה
Psa. 40:6 [1a]Sacrifice and meal offering You have not desired; My ears You have [2]opened; Burnt offering and sin offering You have not required.	לֹא־חָפַצְתָּ אָזְנַיִם כָּרִיתָ לִּי עוֹלָה וַחֲטָאָה לֹא שָׁאָלְתָּ ׃ 8 אָז אָמַרְתִּי הִנֵּה־בָאתִי

7 Then I said, "Behold, I come;
In the scroll of the book it is
[1]written of me.
8 [a]I delight to do Your will, O my
God;
[b]Your Law is within my heart."

Psa. 40:9 I have [a]proclaimed glad
tidings of righteousness in the great
congregation;
Behold, I will [b]not restrain my lips,
O LORD, [c]You know.
10 I have [a]not hidden Your
righteousness within my heart;
I have [b]spoken of Your
faithfulness and Your salvation;
I have not concealed Your
lovingkindness and Your truth from the
great congregation.

Psa. 40:11 You, O LORD, will not
withhold Your compassion from me;
[1]Your [a]lovingkindness and Your
truth will continually preserve me.
12 For evils beyond number have
[a]surrounded me;
My [b]iniquities have overtaken me,
so that I am not able to see;
They are [c]more numerous than the
hairs of my head,
And my [d]heart has [1]failed me.

Psa. 40:13 [a]Be pleased, O LORD, to
deliver me;
Make [b]haste, O LORD, to help me.
14 Let those be [a]ashamed and
humiliated together
Who [b]seek my [1]life to destroy it;
Let those be turned back and
dishonored
Who delight [2]in my hurt.

בִּמְגִלַּת־סֵפֶר כָּתוּב עָלָי ׃
9

לַעֲשׂוֹת־רְצוֹנְךָ אֱלֹהַי
חָפַצְתִּי וְתוֹרָתְךָ בְּתוֹךְ מֵעָי ׃

10 בִּשַּׂרְתִּי צֶדֶק ׀ בְּקָהָל רָב
הִנֵּה שְׂפָתַי לֹא אֶכְלָא יְהֹוָה
אַתָּה יָדָעְתָּ ׃ 11 צִדְקָתְךָ לֹא־
כִסִּיתִי ׀ בְּתוֹךְ לִבִּי אֱמוּנָתְךָ
וּתְשׁוּעָתְךָ אָמָרְתִּי לֹא־
כִחַדְתִּי חַסְדְּךָ וַאֲמִתְּךָ
לְקָהָל רָב ׃ 12 אַתָּה יְהֹוָה
לֹא־תִכְלָא רַחֲמֶיךָ מִמֶּנִּי
חַסְדְּךָ וַאֲמִתְּךָ תָּמִיד
יִצְּרוּנִי ׃ 13 כִּי אָפְפוּ־עָלַי ׀
רָעוֹת עַד־אֵין מִסְפָּר
הִשִּׂיגוּנִי עֲוֹנֹתַי וְלֹא־יָכֹלְתִּי
לִרְאוֹת עָצְמוּ מִשַּׂעֲרוֹת
רֹאשִׁי וְלִבִּי עֲזָבָנִי ׃ 14 רְצֵה
יְהֹוָה לְהַצִּילֵנִי יְהֹוָה
לְעֶזְרָתִי חוּשָׁה ׃ 15 יֵבֹשׁוּ
וְיַחְפְּרוּ ׀ יַחַד מְבַקְשֵׁי נַפְשִׁי
לִסְפּוֹתָהּ יִסֹּגוּ אָחוֹר וְיִכָּלְמוּ
חֲפֵצֵי רָעָתִי ׃ 16 יָשֹׁמּוּ עַל־

15   Let those *a*be ¹appalled because of their shame
    Who *b*say to me, "Aha, aha!"
16   *a*Let all who seek You rejoice and be glad in You;
    Let those who love Your salvation *b*say continually,
    "The LORD be magnified!"
17   Since *c*I am afflicted and needy,
    ¹*b*Let the Lord be mindful of me.
    You are my help and my deliverer;
    Do not delay, O my God.

עֵקֶב בָּשְׁתָּם הָאֹמְרִים לִי הֶאָח ׀ הֶאָח ׃ 17 יָשִׂישׂוּ וְיִשְׂמְחוּ ׀ בְּךָ כָּל־מְבַקְשֶׁיךָ יֹאמְרוּ תָמִיד יִגְדַּל יְהוָה אֹהֲבֵי תְּשׁוּעָתֶךָ ׃ 18 וַאֲנִי ׀ עָנִי וְאֶבְיוֹן אֲדֹנָי יַחֲשָׁב לִי עֶזְרָתִי וּמְפַלְטִי אַתָּה אֱלֹהַי אַל־תְּאַחַר ׃

References

<table>
<tr><td valign="top">

Psalm 40:1
[1]Or *intently*
[a]Ps 25:5; 27:14; 37:7
[b]Ps 34:15

Psalm 40:2
[1]Lit *mud of the mire*
[a]Ps 69:2, 14; Jer 38:6
[b]Ps 27:5
[c]Ps 37:23

Psalm 40:3
[a]Ps 32:7; 33:3
[b]Ps 52:6; 64:9

Psalm 40:4
[1]Lit *regard*
[a]Ps 34:8; 84:12
[b]Job 37:24
[c]Ps 125:5

Psalm 40:5
[a]Job 5:9; Ps 136:4
[b]Ps 139:17; Is 55:8
[c]Ps 71:15; 139:18

Psalm 40:6
[1]I.e. Blood sacrifice
[2]Lit *dug;* or possibly *pierced*
[a]1 Sam 15:22; Ps 51:16; Is 1:11; Jer 6:20; 7:22, 23; Amos 5:22; Mic 6:6-8; Heb 10:5-7

Psalm 40:7
[1]Or *prescribed for*

Psalm 40:8
[a]John 4:34
[b]Ps 37:31; Jer 31:33; 2 Cor 3:3

</td><td valign="top">

Psalm 40:9
[a]Ps 22:22, 25
[b]Ps 119:13
[c]Josh 22:22; Ps 139:4

Psalm 40:10
[a]Acts 20:20, 27
[b]Ps 89:1

Psalm 40:11
[1]Or *May...preserve*
[a]Ps 43:3; 57:3; 61:7; Prov 20:28

Psalm 40:12
[1]Lit *forsaken*
[a]Ps 18:5; 116:3
[b]Ps 38:4; 65:3
[c]Ps 69:4
[d]Ps 73:26

Psalm 40:13
[a]Ps 70:1
[b]Ps 22:19; 71:12

Psalm 40:14
[1]Or *soul*
[2]Or *to injure me*
[a]Ps 35:4, 26; 70:2; 71:13
[b]Ps 63:9

</td></tr>
</table>

<table>
<tr><td>

Psalm 40:15
[1]Or *desolated*
[a]Ps 70:3
[b]Ps 35:21; 70:3

Psalm 40:16
[a]Ps 70:4
[b]Ps 35:27

Psalm 40:17
[1]Or *The Lord is mindful*
[a]Ps 70:5; 86:1; 109:22
[b]Ps 40:5; 1 Pet 5:7

</td><td>

</td></tr>
</table>

Targum

Psa. 40:1 For praise. Of David, a psalm. [2] I truly hoped in the LORD, and he turned to me and received my supplication. [3] And he brought me up from the pit of turmoil, from the mire of filth; and he set my feet on the rock, he made my steps firm. [4] And he put in my mouth a new psalm: Let there be praise before the LORD our God, let many see and fear and hope in the word of the LORD. [5] Happy the man who made the LORD his confidence, and did not look toward the disobedient and those who speak falsehood. [6] Many are the miracles that you have done, O LORD my God; your wonders and favor towards us are impossible to set out; I will recount and speak to you your praise; they are too great to tell. [7] You do not want sacrifice and offering; you have scooped out ears for me to hear your redemption; you have not asked for holocaust and sin offering. [8] Then I said, "Behold, I have entered into eternal life," whenever I occupy myself with the scroll of the book of Torah that was written for my sake. [9] I desire to do your will, O God; and your Torah is contained in my deepest self. [10] I have proclaimed righteousness in the great assembly; behold, I will not withhold my lips; O LORD my God, you know [this]. [11] I have not concealed your righteousness in my heart, I have uttered your truth and your redemption; I have not kept back your goodness and faithfulness in the great assembly. [12] Therefore, you, O LORD, do not withhold your mercy from me; may your goodness and truth always keep me. [13] For evils are strong against me, until they are without number; my sins have overtaken me and I cannot see; they are more numerous than the hairs of my head; and my thoughts have left me. [14] Be pleased, O LORD, to save me; O LORD, hasten to my aid. [15] Those who seek to destroy my soul will be ashamed and confused together; those who desire my ruin will turn back and be disgraced. [16] They will become senseless because of their shame – those who say to me, "We have rejoiced at his ruin, we rejoiced at his misery." [17] All who seek you will rejoice and be glad in your word; and those who love your redemption will say continually, "Let the might of the LORD be magnified." [18] But I am humble and poor, O LORD; let good be devised for me, you are my help and salvation; O my God, do not delay.

Spiritual Awareness

The spiritual rewrite for the verses is in bold.

Introduction

The first eleven verses of this Psalm is a joyous song that David composed when he returned to full health. In the latter part of the Psalm, David speaks about the many dangers that were confronting him.

Superscript

מְנַצֵּחַ (meNatzecha) – means victory. This word is the name of the eighth Sefirah of the Tree of Life. It is not translated in the NASB translation. David called upon the Sefirah Netzach to bring him victory over his enemies. David felt that when he was successful, the LORD was being honored.

To the Sefirah Netzah. A Psalm of David.

Verse one

David hoped for the LORD in the past to help him, and He always did.

I have often hoped for the LORD in the past, striving for Him, and He inclined to hear my cry.

Verse two

שָׁאוֹן (shaon) – means "destruction." This word also denotes a spiritual desolation or spiritual abandonment. David said that the LORD brought him out of his spiritual aloneness.

He raised me up from my spiritual desolation, from the miry mud; He has set my feet upon a rock and firmly established my steps.

Verse three

Since the LORD rose David from his spiritual isolation he wanted to sing a new glorious song to the LORD.

He put a new song in my mouth, a praise to the LORD almighty acts. Many will see and show reverence, and at the same time, learn to trust in the LORD.

Verse four

No matter your situation, King David reminds us always to trust that the LORD is there and will help. All you have to do is ask and have faith.

Forward strides that man who has made when the LORD is the fount of his trust, and has not turned to the arrogant, nor to those who turn away in faithlessness and deceit.

Verse five

David acknowledges the wonderous things that the LORD has done in the Universe.

Many, O LORD my God, are the wonders which You have done, and Your thoughts toward us; There is none to compare with You. If I would declare and speak of them, They would be too numerous to count.

Verse six

The LORD is not looking for sacrifices from those who believed in Him. He is looking for loyal obedience to the Word and a greater sense of duty toward Him. Sacrifices are usually made when a person sins. The LORD is not interested in sin; therefore, the sacrifices are not desired. In other words, do not sin!

You did not desire a meal-offering and sacrifice. You have pierced my ears, You have surely not required ascent-offerings.

Verse seven

David understood that he needed to express his gratitude to the LORD in writing.

So, having contemplated all this, I said: I have come with a written scroll of a book upon me. I understand that I need to express my gratitude with words, both spoken and written.

Verse eight

David said that he was to abandon all his personal desires and accept the Torah in his heart.

To fulfill Your will, my LORD, was my desire, and I accept Your doctrine in my innermost parts.

Verse nine

David immersed himself in the Torah. He came to appreciate it and understand it. He then sought to bring other people to the Torah. He believed that he was obliged to bring the Torah to the people.

I proclaimed righteousness in the great congregation; behold, I shall also not close my lips in the future, O LORD. You know this.

Verse ten

When David proclaimed the destiny of humanity in gatherings, he never concealed what the LORD had done for him. David was guided through the LORD's faithfulness to David and David's faith in the LORD.

I have not hidden Your righteousness within my heart; I have spoken of Your faithfulness and Your salvation; I have not concealed Your lovingkindness and Your truth from the great congregation.

Verse eleven and twelve

The LORD preserved David even when he sinned. Through the Sefirah Chesed, David was forgiven for his sin, and the LORD shined love upon him.

You, O LORD, allowed the Sefirah Chesed to shine upon me. Chesed's love preserved me.

For innumerable evils have beset me once more; my iniquities have overtaken me, and I was no longer able to see; they were more numerous than the hairs on my head, and my heart has failed me.

Verse thirteen to fifteen

David turned to the LORD seeking help because of the sins of the flesh. He prayed for the LORD to deliver him. He also hoped for his enemies to come to know the LORD.

Be pleased, O LORD, to deliver me; Make haste, O LORD, to help me.

Let those be ashamed and humiliated together who seek my [1]life to destroy it; Let those be turned back and dishonored who delight in my hurt.

Let those be appalled because of their shame. Who say to me, "Aha, aha!"

Verse Sixteen

Nothing is as glorious as the LORD. The people who realize that the hand of the LORD is in historical events will receive salvation.

Let all who seek You rejoice and be glad in You; Let those who love Your salvation say continually, "the LORD be magnified!"

Verse seventeen

David acknowledged that he will always need the LORD's help.

Since I am afflicted and needy, let the Lord be mindful of me. You are my help and my deliverer; Do not delay, O my God.

Complete Psalm Rewrite Emphasizing Spiritual Awareness

To the Sefirah Netzah. A Psalm of David.

I have often hoped for the LORD in the past, striving for Him, and He inclined to hear my cry.

He raised me up from my spiritual desolation, from the miry mud; He has set my feet upon a rock and firmly established my steps.

He put a new song in my mouth, a praise to the LORD almighty acts. Many will see and show reverence, and at the same time, learn to trust in the LORD.

Forward strides that man who has made when the LORD is the fount of his trust, and has not turned to the arrogant, nor to those who turn away in faithlessness and deceit.

Many, O LORD my God, are the wonders which You have done, and Your thoughts toward us; There is none to compare with You. If I would declare and speak of them, They would be too numerous to count.
You did not desire a meal-offering and sacrifice. You have pierced my ears, You have surely not required ascent-offerings.

So, having contemplated all this, I said: I have come with a written scroll of a book upon me. I understand that I need to express my gratitude with words, both spoken and written.

To fulfill Your will, my LORD, was my desire, and I accept Your doctrine in my innermost parts.

I proclaimed righteousness in the great congregation; behold, I shall also not close my lips in the future, O LORD. You know this.

I have not hidden Your righteousness within my heart; I have spoken of Your faithfulness and Your salvation; I have not concealed Your lovingkindness and Your truth from the great congregation.
You, O LORD, allowed the Sefirah Chesed to shine upon me. Chesed's love preserved me.

For innumerable evils have beset me once more; my iniquities have overtaken me, and I was no longer able to see; they were more numerous than the hairs on my head, and my heart has failed me.

Be pleased, O LORD, to deliver me; Make haste, O LORD, to help me.

Let those be ashamed and humiliated together who seek my [1]life to destroy it; Let those be turned back and dishonored who delight in my hurt.

Let those be appalled because of their shame. Who say to me, "Aha, aha!"

Let all who seek You rejoice and be glad in You; Let those who love Your salvation say continually, "the LORD be magnified!"
Since I am afflicted and needy, let the Lord be mindful of me. You are my help and my deliverer; Do not delay, O my God.

Appendix

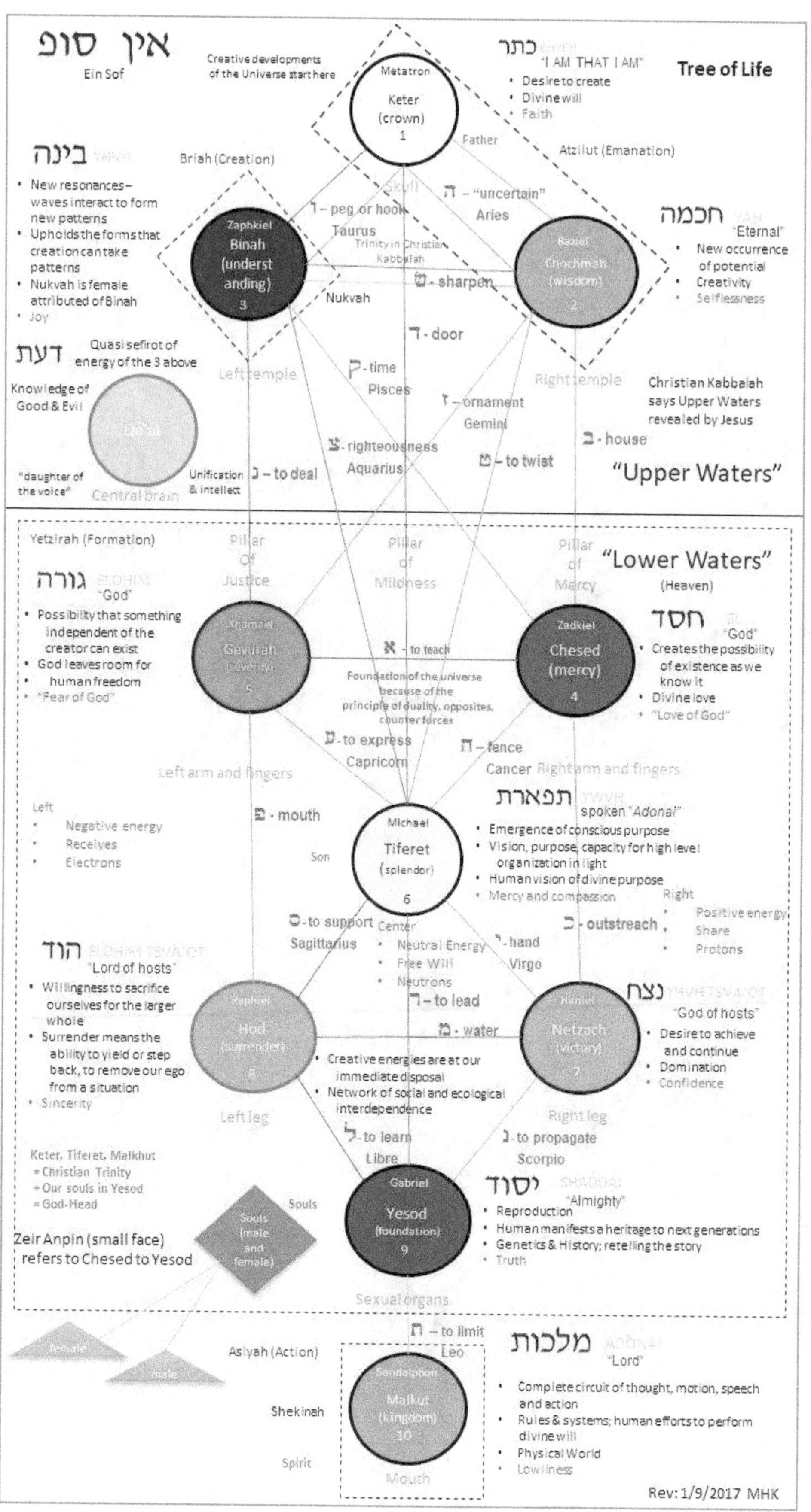

אין סוף
Ein Sof
כתר
"I AM THAT I AM"
• Desire to create
• Divine will
• Faith
Tree of Life
Creative developments of the Universe start here
Metatron
Keter (crown)
1
Father
Briah (Creation)
Atzilut (Emanation)
Skull
ה – "uncertain" Aries
בינה
• New resonances – waves interact to form new patterns
• Upholds the forms that creation can take patterns
• Nukvah is female attributed of Binah
• Joy
ו – peg or hook
Taurus
Trinity in Christian Kabbalah
Zaphkiel
Binah (understanding)
3
ש – sharpen
Nukvah
חכמה
"Eternal"
• New occurrence of potential
• Creativity
• Selflessness
Raziel
Chochmah (wisdom)
2
ד – door
דעת
Quasi sefirot of energy of the 3 above
Knowledge of Good & Evil
ק – time
Pisces
ז – ornament
Gemini
Christian Kabbalah says Upper Waters revealed by Jesus
Daat
"daughter of the voice"
Central brain
Left temple
Right temple
ב – house
צ – righteousness
Aquarius
ל – to deal
ט – to twist
Unification & intellect
"Upper Waters"
Yetzirah (Formation)
Pillar Of Justice
Pillar of Mildness
Pillar of Mercy
"Lower Waters"
(Heaven)
גורה
"God"
• Possibility that something independent of the creator can exist
• God leaves room for human freedom
• "Fear of God"
Khamael
Gevurah (severity)
5
א – to teach
Foundation of the universe because of the principle of duality, opposites, counter forces
חסד
"God"
• Creates the possibility of existence as we know it
• Divine love
• "Love of God"
Zadkiel
Chesed (mercy)
4
מ – to express
Capricorn
ח – fence
Cancer
Left arm and fingers
Right arm and fingers
Left
• Negative energy
• Receives
• Electrons
פ – mouth
Son
Michael
Tiferet (splendor)
6
תפארת
spoken "Adonai"
• Emergence of conscious purpose
• Vision, purpose, capacity for high level organization in light
• Human vision of divine purpose
• Mercy and compassion
Right
• Positive energy
• Share
• Protons
כ – outreach
הוד
"Lord of hosts"
• Willingness to sacrifice ourselves for the larger whole
• Surrender means the ability to yield or step back, to remove our ego from a situation
• Sincerity
ס – to support
Sagittarius
Center
• Neutral Energy
• Free Will
• Neutrons
י – hand
Virgo
נ – to lead
מ – water
נצח
"God of hosts"
• Desire to achieve and continue
• Domination
• Confidence
Raphiel
Hod (surrender)
8
Creative energies are at our immediate disposal
Network of social and ecological interdependence
Haniel
Netzach (victory)
7
Left leg
Right leg
Keter, Tiferet, Malkhut
= Christian Trinity
+ Our souls in Yesod
= God-Head
Zeir Anpin (small face) refers to Chesed to Yesod
ל – to learn
Libre
ג – to propagate
Scorpio
Souls
Souls (male and female)
Gabriel
Yesod (foundation)
9
יסוד
"Almighty"
• Reproduction
• Human manifests a heritage to next generations
• Genetics & History; retelling the story
• Truth
Sexual organs
female
male
ת – to limit
Leo
Asiyah (Action)
מלכות
"Lord"
Sandalphon
Malkut (kingdom)
10
• Complete circuit of thought, motion, speech and action
• Rules & systems; human efforts to perform divine will
• Physical World
• Lowliness
Shekinah
Spirit
Mouth
Rev: 1/9/2017 MHK

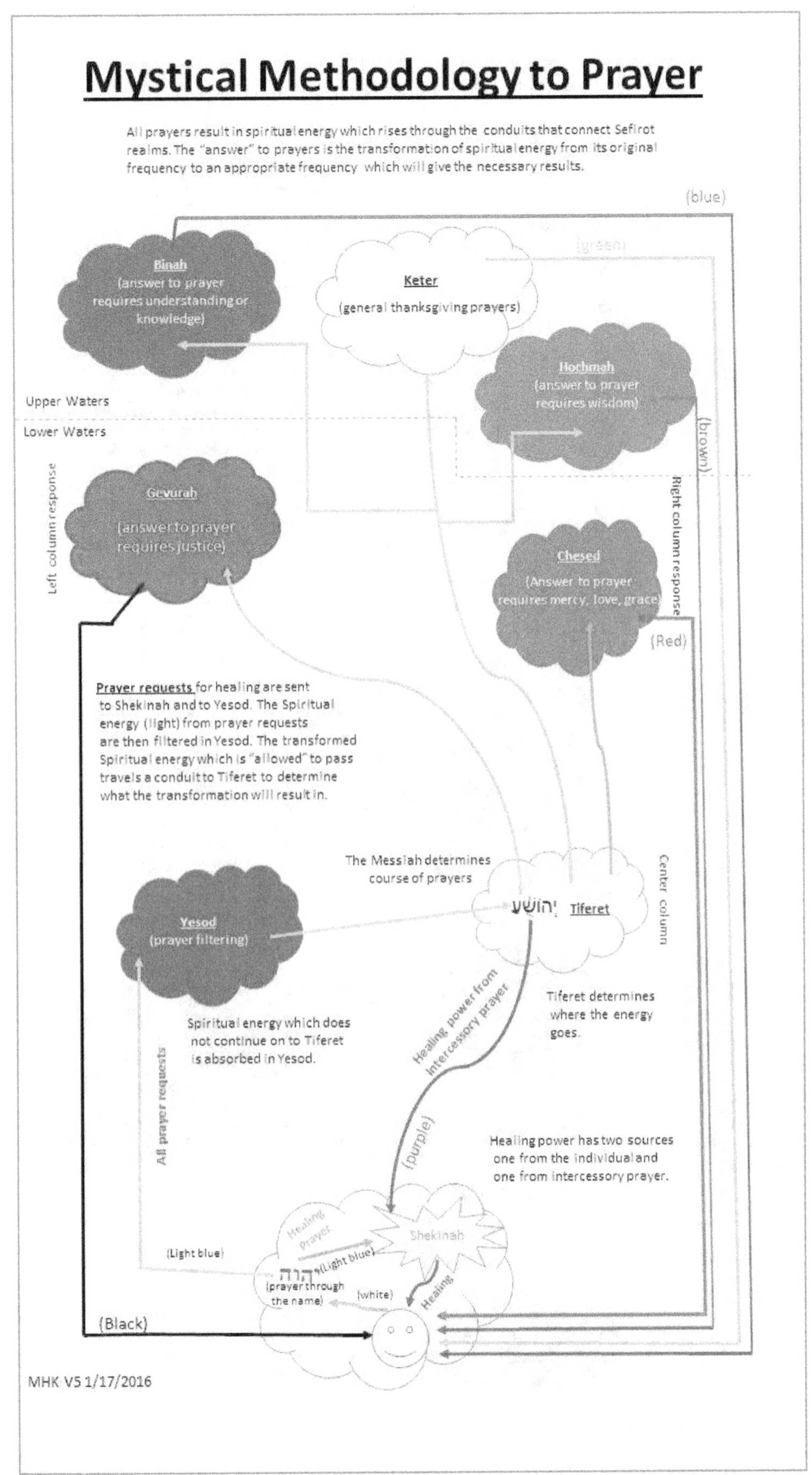

Mystical Methodology to Prayer

All prayers result in spiritual energy which rises through the conduits that connect Sefirot realms. The "answer" to prayers is the transformation of spiritual energy from its original frequency to an appropriate frequency which will give the necessary results.

(blue)
(green)

Binah
(answer to prayer requires understanding or knowledge)

Keter
(general thanksgiving prayers)

Hochmah
(answer to prayer requires wisdom)

(brown)

Upper Waters
Lower Waters

Left column response

Gevurah
(answer to prayer requires justice)

Right column response

Chesed
(Answer to prayer requires mercy, love, grace)

(Red)

Prayer requests for healing are sent to Shekinah and to Yesod. The Spiritual energy (light) from prayer requests are then filtered in Yesod. The transformed Spiritual energy which is "allowed" to pass travels a conduit to Tiferet to determine what the transformation will result in.

The Messiah determines course of prayers

Center column

יהושע Tiferet

Yesod
(prayer filtering)

Tiferet determines where the energy goes.

Spiritual energy which does not continue on to Tiferet is absorbed in Yesod.

Healing power from intercessory prayer

(purple)

Healing power has two sources one from the individual and one from intercessory prayer.

All prayer requests

(Light blue)

Healing Prayer

Shekinah

(Light blue)

יהוה
(prayer through the name)

(white)

Healing

(Black)

MHK V5 1/17/2016

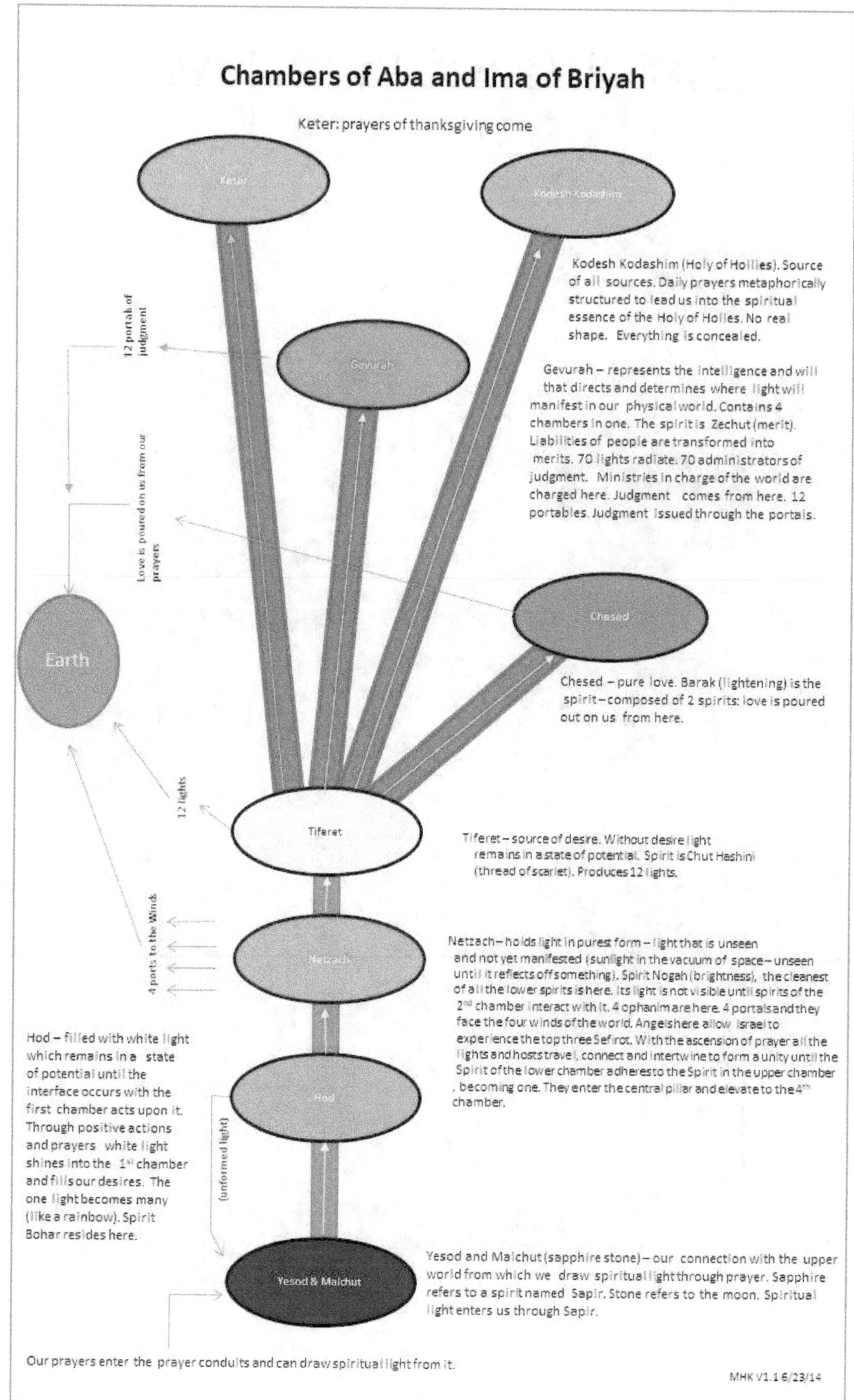

Chambers of Aba and Ima of Briyah

Keter: prayers of thanksgiving come

Keter

Kodesh Kodashim

Gevurah

Chesed

Earth

Tiferet

Netzach

Hod

Yesod & Malchut

12 portals of judgment

Love is poured on us from our prayers

12 lights

4 ports to the Winds

(unformed light)

Kodesh Kodashim (Holy of Hollies). Source of all sources. Daily prayers metaphorically structured to lead us into the spiritual essence of the Holy of Holies. No real shape. Everything is concealed.

Gevurah – represents the intelligence and will that directs and determines where light will manifest in our physical world. Contains 4 chambers in one. The spirit is Zechut (merit). Liabilities of people are transformed into merits. 70 lights radiate. 70 administrators of judgment. Ministries in charge of the world are charged here. Judgment comes from here. 12 portables. Judgment issued through the portals.

Chesed – pure love. Barak (lightening) is the spirit – composed of 2 spirits: love is poured out on us from here.

Tiferet – source of desire. Without desire light remains in a state of potential. Spirit is Chut Hashini (thread of scarlet). Produces 12 lights.

Netzach – holds light in purest form – light that is unseen and not yet manifested (sunlight in the vacuum of space – unseen until it reflects off something). Spirit Nogah (brightness), the cleanest of all the lower spirits is here. Its light is not visible until spirits of the 2nd chamber interact with it. 4 ophanim are here. 4 portals and they face the four winds of the world. Angels here allow Israel to experience the top three Sefirot. With the ascension of prayer all the lights and hosts travel, connect and intertwine to form a unity until the Spirit of the lower chamber adheres to the Spirit in the upper chamber, becoming one. They enter the central pillar and elevate to the 4th chamber.

Hod – filled with white light which remains in a state of potential until the interface occurs with the first chamber acts upon it. Through positive actions and prayers white light shines into the 1st chamber and fills our desires. The one light becomes many (like a rainbow). Spirit Bohar resides here.

Yesod and Malchut (sapphire stone) – our connection with the upper world from which we draw spiritual light through prayer. Sapphire refers to a spirit named Sapir. Stone refers to the moon. Spiritual light enters us through Sapir.

Our prayers enter the prayer conduits and can draw spiritual light from it.

MHK V1.1 6/23/14

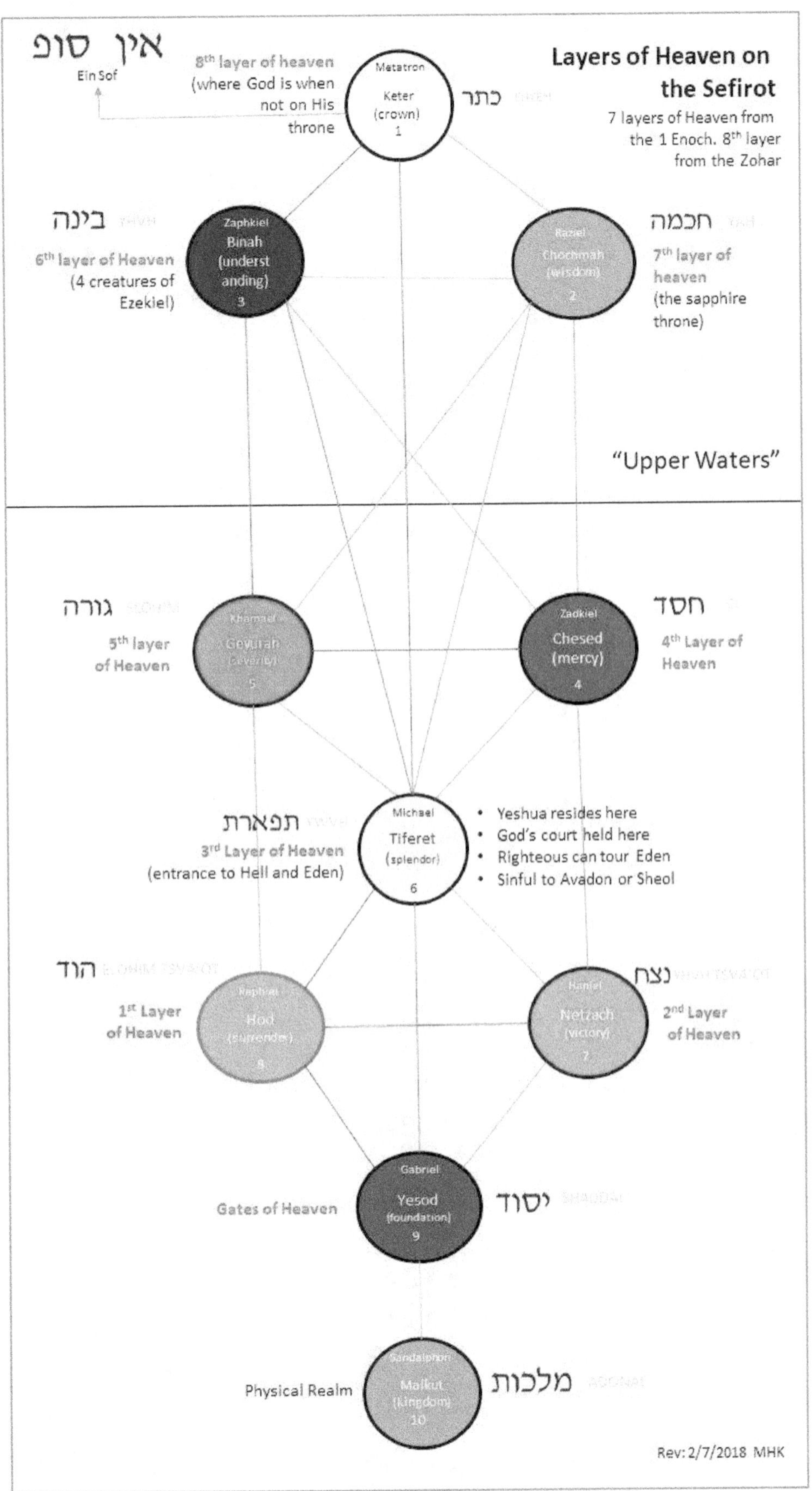
אין סוף
Ein Sof

8th layer of heaven (where God is when not on His throne)

Matatron
Keter (crown)
1

כתר

Layers of Heaven on the Sefirot
7 layers of Heaven from the 1 Enoch. 8th layer from the Zohar

בינה
6th layer of Heaven (4 creatures of Ezekiel)

Zaphkiel
Binah (understanding)
3

Raziel
Chochmah (wisdom)
2

חכמה
7th layer of heaven (the sapphire throne)

"Upper Waters"

גורה
5th layer of Heaven

Khamael
Gevurah (severity)
5

Zadkiel
Chesed (mercy)
4

חסד
4th Layer of Heaven

תפארת
3rd Layer of Heaven (entrance to Hell and Eden)

Michael
Tiferet (splendor)
6

• Yeshua resides here
• God's court held here
• Righteous can tour Eden
• Sinful to Avadon or Sheol

הוד
1st Layer of Heaven

Raphael
Hod (surrender)
8

Haniel
Netzach (victory)
7

נצח
2nd Layer of Heaven

Gabriel
Yesod (foundation)
9

Gates of Heaven

יסוד

Sandalphon
Malkut (kingdom)
10

Physical Realm

מלכות

Rev: 2/7/2018 MHK